BROKEN SILENCE

BROKEN SILENCE

Opening Your Heart and Mind to Therapy— A Black Woman's Recovery Guide

D. KIM SINGLETON, ED.D.

ONE WORLD
BALLANTINE BOOKS · NEW YORK

A One World Book

Published by The Random House Ballantine Publishing Group

Copyright © 2003 by D. Kim Singleton, Ed.D.

Scripture quotations marked (KJV) are taken from the Holy Bible, King James Version.

The Scripture quotation marked (NLT) is taken from the Holy Bible, New Living Translation, copyright © 1996. Used by permission of Tyndale House Publishers, Inc., Wheaton, Illinois 60189. All rights reserved.

ISBN 0-345-44644-5

Text design by Kris Tobiassen

Manufactured in the United States of America

To my sister, Geraldine Enright Finch,
and
my daughter, Kimberly C. Singleton

Happy is the person who finds wisdom
and gains understanding.
For the profit of wisdom is better than silver,
and her wages are better than gold.

—PROVERBS 3:13–14 (NLT)

Contents

Acknowledgments

THE UNCONDITIONAL LOVE, ENCOURAGEMENT, AND SUP-
port of my family have always made me want to be a better person. The reviews, suggestions, and challenges from my husband,
William C. Singleton II ("Sing"), stimulated my thoughts and
helped me to be clear. I am indebted to my daughter, Kimberly C.
Singleton, for her support and the resources she provided through
Sing-Sing 2000 Entertainment. The quiet strength and support
of my sister, Geraldine Enright Finch, were always available to
me. My sons and daughters: William C. III and Nichole Singleton, Marc K. and Carla Singleton; and grandsons William C. IV
and Cameron C. Singleton and Harry Croxton Jr. gave of themselves to make sure I stayed on target.

I am grateful for the guidance from my literary agent,
Lawrence Jordan, and editor Anita Diggs. Thanks to the Ballantine staff for taking me through the door.

Many, many thanks to my families, friends, and colleagues
who encouraged and waited patiently with me for *Broken Silence*
to be published. For their prayers, encouragement, and support, I

offer special thanks to Sisterfriend Rev. Angeloyd Bolar Fenrick, Joseph C. Fenrick Jr., Gloria Watts Davis, and Joyce W. Alexander; and to my pastor, Rev. Dr. Henry P. Davis III, and church family at the First Baptist Church of Highland Park in Landover, Maryland, and Rev. Robert Boyd Hunter, rector, and church family at the Atonement Episcopal Church in Washington, D.C.

There is a special place in my heart for the eight women in this book and the other Black women who shared their stories with me through the years. Without them, this book would not have been possible.

These are true stories. However, all names, identifying characteristics, and other details of the case material, including journal entries, questionnaires, and letters, have been changed to protect the identity of the women.

BROKEN
SILENCE

Introduction

I SAW THE T-SHIRT WHEN I WAS RUMMAGING THROUGH THE clutter on a street vendor's stand one morning. The words on it jumped out at me: BEING A BLACK WOMAN IS ONE OF THE HARDEST JOBS IN THE WORLD. I stopped and stared at them for a long time. As a Black woman, the message touched me deeply. As a psychologist, I thought of all the Black women whom I had talked with and listened to over the past fifteen years. It was as if someone had peered into our collective unconscious and understood our dilemma. I recalled the themes and issues and remembered the tears and the pain. I heard the cries: *I'm hurting; I just want the pain to go away; What's wrong with me?; I'm lonely; Try to understand me.*

In order to find relief, these women used sex, work, and food in unhealthy ways. A few added alcohol or drugs to the mix. Others sought refuge in religion or by consulting psychics. Almost all hid behind walls of silence. Only when the pain and pressure from financial, family, or personal crises became overwhelming did the women turn to therapy for help.

In therapy (short for *psychotherapy*), a trained mental health professional assists us in talking out our problems in a private setting so we can explore the possible causes of the problems and either come to terms with or overcome them. Since therapy is a specialty mental health service, each session is considered confidential.

There are various types of psychotherapists. Please refer to "Resources" in the back of the book for a thorough definition of each.

The goal of therapy is to achieve the clarity and balance we need to be effective and happy. When we are effective and happy in our lives, we restore our personal power. When our personal power is lost, whether someone steals it or we give it away, we are open to manipulation and control by other people. They push our buttons, choose for us, and direct our lives as we yield to them. Using professional help to restore personal power is not a weakness. Rather, it is acknowledgment that competent, objective assistance is available beyond the usual help of family and friends. In therapy, we learn to understand the "what" and "why" in our lives, giving us the choice to act in constructive ways.

In therapy, the entire focus is on the women seeking help. This is one of the significant differences between seeking professional help and getting advice from close family members and friends. With family and friends, the focus of concerns and problems often shifts between individuals. (Remember all the times you started to talk about a problem with a friend or family member and she interrupted to talk about a similar problem before you finished?) Regardless, each is concerned about the other's personal happiness or preferences, and the exchange can extend over a lifetime.

In therapy, the women did not have to be concerned about my happiness or preferences. The setting provided a safe, objective place for the women to work exclusively on themselves.

Black women's use of therapy as a resource to help with problems in our lives is relatively new. Many are still unfamiliar with therapy as a treatment for life problems, and others wonder why a sane person would seek it. There is the stigma that therapy is for "crazy people," but also, seeking professional help implies an admission of weakness and vulnerability that defies the *strong Black woman* stereotypes some of us have internalized.

Yet, when we consider that therapy is a professional relationship that encourages people to discuss the most intimate details of their lives with a complete stranger and pay for it, it's reasonable that therapists and the process may be viewed with suspicion. Self-disclosure is basic to the therapeutic process, but historically it has not always worked in Black people's favor. Well-documented accounts of slavery, "Jim Crow" laws and segregation, and the Civil Rights Movements provide examples of how disclosed information about Black people seeking freedom and equality was used to create unpleasant work and social situations, and caused others to be beaten or killed.

Black Therapist versus White Therapist

Self-disclosure surfaces as an issue in the Black-therapist-versus-White-therapist discussion. Therapists are trained to perform helping functions, the success of which depends a great deal on relationship factors. A good relationship implies some degrees of interest, liking, acceptance, trust, honesty, understanding, and caring. Historically, the relationship between Blacks and Whites in the United States has been permeated with distrust due to racism in all of its facets. This sense of distrust does not necessarily end in the therapist's office. Therapists—Black or White—do not automatically turn into magical, loving, unbiased creatures just because they are therapists. Therapists are essentially the same persons within and outside of therapeutic sessions.

Perception and understanding of experiences are issues in the Black-therapist-versus-White-therapist discussion. Talking is a primary component in therapy. Through it, personal information, perspectives, and experiences are revealed. Therapists listen to their clients to get the full meaning of the messages. Unfortunately, White therapists do not always understand what their Black clients are saying. Consequently, relationship building is seriously impaired when Black women must explain to White therapists the meanings and nuances in the Black experience so that the therapist can grasp the depth of the concerns presented. To do so is frustrating, tiring, and too much work.

While it is possible for some White therapists to function effectively in therapy with Black people, they cannot assume that it will happen automatically. It takes willingness and effort to understand frames of reference outside their own.

Resistance to Therapy

Culturally, therapy is not the usual way that Black women solve problems. Instead, family, friends, and the church help with personal, financial, legal, and health problems or racism issues, and resistance to therapy is common. Exceptions occur when families have reached the end with members who have serious psychological issues or who have become serious threats to themselves or the people around them. When this happens, a hospital or institution is usually considered. Many of us associate therapy with these extreme situations.

Black women also resist therapy due to its cost. Money is limited for most women. To some, paying a stranger to talk about problems does not make any sense. It seems a waste when the money can be used on basics, like food and shelter, or more tangible and desirable things, like beauty care, clothes, or a car.

While fees for therapy per session may range from $65 to $150, some therapists offer sliding scales based upon your income. Many health insurance plans cover some percentage of therapy costs with a small co-pay or, in some instances, all costs when the therapists in their network are used. Therapy is also available at no cost through company-sponsored employee assistance programs.

Religion and the church play major roles in some of our lives. They help us deal with forces and powers beyond our control and give us emotional support. Beliefs in God, "a higher power," Christianity, and other religions are sources of strength. They counteract the adverse life experiences that could lead to illness.

Black women often resist therapy because we think or feel that it betrays our religious beliefs. It is common to hear, "I take my problems to the Lord!" We rely on spiritual foundations and biblical teachings to guide and sustain us through problems. Within this context, using therapy implies inadequate faith in God. When this judgment is supported by the church, it often breeds guilt, making us feel like traitors who are abandoning our faith. Consequently, women mask their pain and remain silent and hurting. They do not realize both therapy and the church are legitimate resources.

Church social norms are also factors in our resistance to therapy. Our churches accept us. We are free to worship in our own styles and release our emotions and distress. The experience strengthens us to cope with the stressors of everyday life. In the past and now, the recognition, respect, and refuge from hostile environments that we receive in the Black church provide a safety net that nurtures our mental health.

Traditionally, Black churches have advised members to find answers to life's problems exclusively in prayer, but growing numbers of clergy are recognizing that therapy is helpful. They support the work of mental health professionals in their congregations and community and sometimes refer members to them.

Beyond the spiritual implications of church affiliation, there are opportunities to have companionship, form lasting friendships, and participate in social events that may be unavailable in other settings. The events include dinners, plays, bazaars, and birthday gatherings. Some churches sponsor dances that women attend comfortably without male escorts. Although it is typical to find more African American women than men in church, at times women meet men and form romantic liaisons that result in marriage.

Resistance to therapy also comes from the mental health system itself. The system has the power to penalize us by the judgments it makes about our mental fitness, whether these judgments are valid or not.

I, too, resisted therapy. Becoming a therapist was not a childhood dream. In fact, the only people I knew in therapy while growing up were those committed to the state mental hospital. Vaguely, I remember going there as a child with my mother, a church missionary who visited a neighbor confined in the facility. My playmates and I called it the crazy house—a perception that stretched into my early teens. My attitude changed only as I learned more about mental health services in high school and college from professionals in the field. Even then, however, trust was an issue.

As a doctoral student in training, participation in therapy was required to help me experience the process and work through personal issues that might interfere with my role as a helping professional. I entered therapy reluctantly. Judging that it was not a safe place, I disclosed hardly anything significant—sometimes nothing at all. My thoughts said, *Keep your business to yourself; this person is not your friend.* Experience with racism and discrimination blurred my view of my White male therapist as a caring, trustworthy person.

We both struggled through the sessions, and most were fruitless, because I was too guarded to participate fully. My impenetrable resistance frustrated and irritated him. His attempts to pick and probe into my family life and background, issues, and feelings got on my nerves. Thinking increasingly that this therapy was not all it was touted to be, I decided to go along with it to complete the requirements, graduate, and get on with my life as I had planned.

Our dance ended only when fatigue forced me to use the process to look at the school and time management issues overwhelming me and accept help in resolving them. The therapist's questions, comments, and self-disclosure led me to see how critical the need was to take care of myself with rest and relaxation. I blocked his attempts to probe deeper into my life because I didn't trust him and felt like a guinea pig when he required too much explanation to understand what he wanted to know. My experience in therapy helped me to realize that without trust, building a relationship is difficult.

Themes in Therapy

Career concerns, dissatisfying relationships, and childhood and adult abuse emerge as frequent themes in therapy. These themes reflect the contradictions and insensitivity Black women live with daily because of who we are and how we have been defined. In the past and now, Black women know that gender and color carry penalties. In our society, these instantly recognizable traits create barriers that severely limit our opportunities and social acceptability, as well as our access to material goods and positions of power and authority.

Sexism and racism taunt our very existence. Low wages, limited advancement, and isolation are ever-present career concerns. According to the U.S. Census Bureau, while 78 percent of Black women twenty-five or more years old held high school diplomas or college degrees by 2000, they were primarily employed in service occupations or as operators, fabricators, and laborers.

Economic discrimination and limited jobs are particularly challenging when the American Dream is paraded before us while numbers of Black women, with and without children, struggle with poverty. Census figures also tell us that of the estimated eight million Black people living below the poverty level, five million are Black women. More than a few Black women live with built-in expectations that they must work not only to support themselves but also to help family members financially. In marriage, there are Black women who are not surprised to find their salaries the primary income. They sustain the family financially or maintain a given lifestyle.

Racism and sexism do not explain all of Black women's negative life experiences, but their lightning bolts constantly strike our minds, bodies, and spirits. Paired, racism and sexism are key environmental factors that make our life experiences different from those of White and Black males and White females. White males make the rules that affect every other group. Black males deal with the resulting institutional racism. White females encounter sexism. Black females endure both.

Influences

Relationships with fathers or significant male figures influence how women relate to the men in their lives. During our formative years of early childhood, fathers or male role models teach us

how men behave, what to expect from them, and how to respond to them. The nature of those relationships forms our later
responses to men. In healthy, nurturing relationships, we learn to
respond in wholesome ways. In unhealthy relationships, we learn
to respond in unwholesome ways. Unhealthy responses cause
distress and dissatisfaction.

Abusive experiences teach women to expect to be treated
poorly. Black women of all ages are victimized by rape, sexual assault, robbery, and aggravated and simple assault. A 2001 Department of Justice special report by Callie M. Rennison tells us that
between 1993 and 1999, intimate partner violence against Black
women was 19 victimizations per 1,000 for females ages 16
through 19; 29 per 1,000 for females ages 20 through 24; and 16
per 1,000 for females ages 25 through 34. Many tolerate poor
treatment hoping that if they hold out long enough, the negative
behavior will stop. It is a symptom of low self-esteem: Women
feel unworthy of love and stay in abusive situations trying to
make themselves more appealing. The prospect of not having a
man in their lives intimidates others, and they submit to mistreatment rather than go it alone.

Black women in therapy often revealed their abuse to me
during an exploration of relationships in which we used family
tree charts to probe periods in their lives they could not remember. Preparing the charts stimulated their memories and released
them to talk about hidden people, places, and events. Most had
told no one about the abuse before entering therapy. After Oprah
Winfrey revealed her childhood sexual abuse, a rush of twenty-

to thirty-five-year-old Black women came into my office to talk about theirs.

One young woman expressed a widespread sentiment when she told of molestations at age ten by her cousin's husband during visits to their home. "I thought I did something to make him bother me. Mother said I had a crush on him. I thought if I told her, she would say I did something to make him act that way toward me. So, I just buried it. It was my deep, dark secret."

The violations of the women in my practice usually occurred when they were seven to eleven years old, though some were younger and others older. Mothers' boyfriends, stepfathers, uncles, cousins, male friends of the family, brothers and stepbrothers, and some biological fathers committed the acts. Less often, female relatives and family friends were the abusers. Older women in therapy generally took their childhood sexual abuse in stride as something that happened to any Black girl growing up. Feeling powerless, they blocked it out. Their sexual abuse was not always a secret, but nobody talked about it.

As I searched my own past, an incident that happened when I was twelve years old popped vividly into my mind. Twice a month, I played the piano for morning and afternoon services at a small rural church. On the usual drive home one Sunday night, the minister—a thirty-eight-year-old family friend—took a detour and parked on an isolated street. He didn't say anything when I asked why he stopped but leaned over to kiss me. I pushed his head away while blurting a few expletives my mother didn't know I knew, insisting that he take me home immediately. He started the car but before he finished asking if I was going to tell, my shouts filled the car. We were silent for the remainder of the trip home.

My father stood at his usual front-door spot waiting for me. After hearing my story, he left immediately to confront the man but never found him. We learned later that he left town after dropping me off. I was fortunate the man hadn't threatened, hit, or raped me. His history of sexual molestation surfaced as girls and young women came forward to describe how he had accosted them as well.

Themes of careers, relationships, and abuse recurred in stories of the more than forty-five hundred Black women I have seen in therapy over the last fifteen years as a licensed clinical psychologist. The same themes emerged during the "Helping the Hurting" and "What You Need to Know Before You Marry" workshops I led. These stories were so frequent and similar that only the names of the women telling them changed. I felt compelled to look closer to find effective ways to help my clients.

Broken Silence: Opening Your Heart and Mind to Therapy—A Black Woman's Recovery Guide offers an overview of the cultural norms that have shaped and bruised Black femininity and examines the lives of eight African American women who turned to therapy to deal with their pain. In the course of their work with me, career disappointments, failed relationships, and childhood and adult abuse were revealed. I chose these eight women because their stories capture both the essence of the struggles faced by countless Black women and their apprehensions about using therapy to help them. The eight women show that it is possible and safe to confront painful issues and events in therapy and create more satisfying results in their lives.

The stories in *Broken Silence* help us to understand how past events in our lives influence our present behavior; knowing this, we can use the information to make better choices. They also provide a channel of communication to women who need to know they are not alone in their experiences, and to men who want to understand why some women behave in the ways they do.

The Eight Women

Chapter 2, "First Visits," and chapter 3, "They Fired Me," reflect not only the discrimination experienced by Black women but also our resistance to therapy. "First Visits" unveils May's struggle with her pain, loneliness, and quality of life. Trapped and made helpless by inexperience, May does not know her emotional options or how to generate them. Like inhaled smoke, negative emotions fill her inner space and feed on themselves. Guilt, frustration, fear, and insecurity overwhelm her.

Pain drove May into therapy, but she is uneasy about anyone finding out that she has sought help. Her mental message says, *Therapy is for crazy people,* and she does not want people to think she is crazy. Despite her apprehension, though, she acts to ease her distress. As May comes to understand how life events have influenced her present behavior, she releases the negative emotions and learns effective new responses.

When employers deny promotions to, demote, or fire Black women, the loss of income, position, and status create pain. These setbacks increase levels of emotional distress, particularly for women who bear the major financial responsibility for themselves and their families. Many strain to meet financial obligations and often sacrifice their own needs to do for the people in their lives. Victoria is one of these women.

Victoria's pride and need for help collide with resistance to therapy in "They Fired Me." Along with the isolation she faces on her job, Victoria has sole financial responsibility for her family and must deal with a pressing health issue. Prolonged stressful situations like Victoria's are often associated with the onset of depression and physical illness. With changes in her attitude and behavior, however, she turns her difficulties into opportunities to succeed.

The complexities and impenetrable boundaries Black women face in career movement are seen in chapter 4, "Steel Ceilings, Not Glass." It looks at Nora's frustrations with the pressures of her job in private industry, where subtle and blatant racism and sexism remind her that the struggle for equity persists. She focuses on coping strategies and the support she needs to survive.

Chapter 5, "Cleaning Up My Act," explores Kate's unhealthy behavior in relationships. Being without a man is a prominent concern for her. Kate—along with many women, of all ages—laments the lack of suitable ways and places to meet men who are interested in building monogamous relationships, friendships, or marriages.

Kate is typical of women who surrender their identity and power to other people for acceptance and love. She enters therapy to reclaim both. In exploring her relationships with men, we look at attitudes, expectations, and sexual behavior as factors that have influenced the quality of her relationships. Kate makes her connections, then is able to restore her power by choosing how she will function in her relationships with men.

Like Kate, some women view marriage as a solution to their relationship problems without recognizing the work required to sustain and make it successful. Some view marriage as a solution to their problems, period. Others are not interested in marriage. Meeting and bonding as compatible companions is a satisfactory alternative for them.

In chapter 6, "I Don't Think He Loves Me Anymore," themes of aging and loss of affection surface when sixty-two-year-old Maggie enters therapy for depression and anxiety. Her spouse's indifference and unexplained negative changes in behavior threaten her. Fear of being alone undermines Maggie's confidence, but she slowly comes to look within herself for acceptable alternatives. Lifestyle changes affirm her hidden abilities and increase her self-esteem.

Physical abuse often follows emotional abuse. Chapter 7, "Too Ashamed to Tell," recounts Ava's almost fatal experience in a relationship where intimidation and fear reigned. She has sacrificed her emotional well-being, in part, for financial security because Ava enjoys the advantages of two incomes and doubts her ability to live solely on her own salary. Socially isolated and embarrassed by her husband's behavior toward her, her friends, and her family, she seeks help in therapy. There she comes to terms with her pain and offers advice to women in similar relationships.

The abuse women experience as children and adults has its own language: drooped shoulders, drawn faces with no hints of laughter, and sad or angry eyes. The eyes are the most telling. The distant, cheerless gaze penetrates beyond its immediate path without sparkle. Pam and Amy are two such women. Both were sexually abused as children.

Pam and Amy are from different economic and educational backgrounds, but their experiences have very similar effects on them. The violations stole their childhood innocence and chipped away at their self-esteem. The violators left *I-do-not-value-you* messages and reference points from which the women judged themselves as unworthy of love. Their stories explore the continuing impact of childhood sexual abuse and how they worked through it. Both women examine themselves and their relationships with males and family members to reclaim their power and reorder their lives.

In chapter 8, "Stolen Innocence," twenty-six-year-old Pam faces shame, guilt, and fear of intimacy from her abuse and silence about it. Her veiled cries for help go unnoticed, and emotional scars follow Pam into adulthood to influence her expectations of herself and others. She enters therapy to work through these emotional issues; as her confidence grows, she's able to make changes in her lifestyle and relationships.

The negative effects of unhealthy family dynamics deepen when Amy's biological father molests her. Chapter 9, "Behind

Closed Doors," looks at her response to the abuse and the trust and abandonment issues that result. Amy and her mother recognize that their behavior is influenced by parental modeling and try to build a better relationship.

Each of the eight women in this book started the healing process when she confronted the traumatic events in her life. Breaking the silence was a major step in coming to terms with pain and humiliation. The women removed the cloaks of silence over long-held secrets and other stresses. They told what happened to them, how the events influenced their lives, and how they managed. To tell was a new and difficult behavior because these women, like many of us, had been reared to keep their business to themselves. Difficult, also, because they assumed that their silence protected loved ones from being impacted.

Silence and reluctance to tell are related to safety issues and the risks involved in self-disclosure. What happens when we tell? Who is interested and will take our concerns seriously? Who can and will do anything about them? Who is there to tell, particularly when the protectors are also the violators?

In therapy with the women, I assume they have lost some or all of their personal power—and that we can restore it. Since I know they have the capacity to choose, think, and feel, I focus immediately on those properties when we meet. This attitude of acceptance and positive regard sets the tone for our journey and taps into their responsibility to be active participants in the process. We seek clarity in everything because it leads to wise choices.

Understanding how attitudes influence the quality of results helps us achieve clarity and balance. Attitudes include the mind-sets that dictate how much we invest in ourselves, other people, and situations. They include, also, clarity about our expectations—those mental pictures of what we see happening with the people, events, and situations in our lives. Clear expectations reduce conflict.

Goals of This Book

One goal of *Broken Silence* is to furnish clear explanations, practical suggestions, and exercises that women can apply to their lives. Another is to provide information about the symptoms that may motivate hurting women to seek professional help for emotional pain. Physical and emotional injuries issue varying degrees of pain that can drastically alter the quality of our lives. We get treatment for physical injuries because they are visible and harder to ignore or hide. Emotional injuries are just as devastating and painful but are less likely to be treated because they are invisible.

While some stress keeps us alert and productive, prolonged distress causes changes in the body that lower our resistance to illness. Extensive medical research on the relationship between psychological stress and physical health links some illnesses—such as ulcers, heart disease, and high blood pressure—to stress. Multiple roles and the combination of job pressure and emotional isolation may well be major factors in the rates of disease and premature death suffered by Black women, especially those who bear additional weights from high-profile, high-pressure positions.

The world today is complex, chaotic, dehumanizing, and

dangerous. We see the results in human interactions characterized by irresponsible behavior, dishonesty, personal distress, and acts of violence. Emotional healing begins by recognizing the need to get help. Burdens can be lifted and solutions found when we set aside time to work through our problems with someone who is trained, competent, and caring.

Therapy, sometimes called the "talking cure," is a viable resource to address the problems we face. The structured, therapeutic setting is designed to be a safe place for empathy, comfort, and growth. An additional benefit is the insight we gain about ourselves and our impact on others. Since participants, like therapists, bring the same behavior into the therapeutic setting that they show outside of it, decisions can be made on how to change the behavior that occurs in therapy sessions.

Emotional healing comes with awareness that choice is always an option. Even when daily events influence our lives in ways that seem almost impossible to escape, we can still choose to shape meaningful responses to our life situations. Our authority to choose is personal power. It is one of our strongest forces.

Throughout my years as a mental health professional, I witnessed Black women's consistent silence about disturbing life issues, taking care of other people, and tolerance for pain. I understood because I had acted the same way. However, as I worked in school and university settings, vocational rehabilitation and Veterans Administration facilities, churches, and government agencies, I increasingly began to value the therapeutic process as a source in gaining a new understanding of ourselves as Black women.

I began to understand that acceptance, honesty, and listening are crucial elements needed to build a relationship and promote positive results. Acceptance means providing space for persons to be who they are in their thinking, feeling, and actions—acknowledging that it is all right for them to be there.

My wish to make therapy more accessible to Black women led me to the private practice of psychology where our issues and mood and anxiety disorders are addressed. My vision included awareness that women can assign positive values to therapy when they understand what it is and actively participate. So my practice generally begins with demystifying the therapeutic process by educating women about it. This involves making plain what to expect from the process; determining what they want to happen in our time together and whether or not we can achieve it; and clarifying what they can do to create positive results.

I encourage writing in a journal to help women heal and grow. The journal is an unbiased ear to hear those thoughts and emotions that otherwise would be locked in our heads and hearts. It is also a mirror to reflect our inner self. Journal writing allows us to sort and release feelings, provides a perspective to view progress, and binds the time between therapy visits.

I don't use the word *patient* to describe the women who come to me because the term implies the kind of deficiency that society continually reinforces. I do not see them in that way. Beginning from a position of strength, on the other hand, nourishes and encourages women to recognize that they can achieve goals and restore their personal power.

I learned a lot about both other Black women and myself

during therapy. I saw myself reflected in them and them in me. We learned from each other as I walked with them through the therapeutic process. The quality of the interactions set the tone for self-esteem to grow. A relationship built on mutual respect supported the women as they improved the quality of their lives.

In writing *Broken Silence*, I want Black women to know we are not isolated in our experiences. The same and similar things happen to all of us because of the ways we have been defined in society. It is time to break the silence and move to higher levels of self-awareness so that our suppressed talents can be released to make the world a better place. I want women to see therapy as a resource to do this; to start a new tradition by using it and knowing that it is okay. Therapy allows the freedom to clear away cobwebs and make room for redefinition. It is all a part of taking care of ourselves. I want women to give themselves permission to take care of themselves without guilt.

May, Victoria, Nora, Kate, Maggie, Pam, Ava, and Amy show us that change is possible. They learned to change themselves and, in turn, change the way others responded to them. They illustrate ways to use information to develop different, more satisfying courses of action. These women help us reconnect with our power to change.

Broken Silence accurately conveys the themes that were most central in the lives of certain Black women in therapy. All names, identifying characteristics of the individuals mentioned in this book, and other details of the case material, journal entries, and letters have been changed to protect their privacy.

ONE

Legacies

SOCIETY'S STEREOTYPICAL VIEW OF OUR FOREMOTHERS as strong, subservient, emotionless breeders placed tremendous weights on them and succeeding female generations.

Slave women took care of White women and their households, husbands, and children while taking care of their own children, often fathered by White slave masters. Often, the demands of attending to White women kept them from their loved ones entirely. When the enslaved children and adults were split up and moved to other plantations, slave women cared for the extended families that remained.

The primary role of taking care of other people was one that our foremothers could not change or escape. To do so invited punishment or even death. The inability to protect their own children and keep their families together added to the emotional and physical pain they already bore in silence. Moreover, slave women did not have the luxury of "time out" to grieve their losses and heal from the offenses doled out. They had to keep moving in hostile environments, fulfilling the responsibilities thrust upon them.

Being oppressed and trapped in a society that heralded women as the fairer sex, yet denied Black women the perks of being female, was one of the many contradictions that flooded our foremothers' lives. The image of marriage as a haven where women stayed at home to be cared for financially and emotionally was not an option that slave status permitted. Black women performed the same tasks as slave men, in addition to their other duties.

Society characterized women as soft, weak, and cultured but treated slave women as tough, strong, and coarse. All that was touted as physically beautiful and desirable was the opposite of the average Black woman's characteristics. Slave women worked as asexual beings but were sexually assaulted at the same time.

As society abused them, slave women developed defenses to help them survive and cushion the abuse. The illusion of being needed and valued by owners linked self-worth with service to others: *If I'm needed to take care of others and keep things going, I must be of some value.* Doing for others also taught slave women to fix things. Without resources, they were usually left to make something out of nothing. Fixing gave them a sense of control and power over at least some external influences.

Slavery left the indelible legacies of taking-care-of-others, silence, and tolerance-for-pain that Black women experience to this day. They have affected how we think, act, and feel about ourselves.

We take care of others before considering our own needs. In

doing so, we are forever trying to fix. If we can fix it, we can deal with it. We appear able to handle situations because we have always had to and feel locked into doing so. Others in our world know they only have to wait before we become impatient at something *not* getting done. It's our *if-I-don't-do-it, it-won't-get-done* mentality. Assuming responsibility to make something better adds another item to our ever-expanding list of things to do, even when we are already overwhelmed.

Silence and masked feelings were survival tactics that helped our foremothers to stay alive. The slave status that forced them into hard labor and into taking care of their owners' sexual needs also forced them into silence about their abuse because they had no rights or protectors.

Family relationships help us to further understand the legacy of silence. Family systems are our sources of support, advice, help, and protection unavailable anywhere else. When something goes wrong within the family, then, there are few places to turn. Silence becomes a mantle of protection hiding fear, guilt, and shame. It helps us to manage conflicting emotions, particularly in cases of emotional, sexual, or physical abuse where the same person is both violator and protector. Revealing abuse is threatening because it makes everyone vulnerable, but when no one tells, the impact of the abusive acts remains hidden.

And silence extends even deeper into our psyche to issues of self-disclosure, trust, and vulnerability. Making ourselves known by revealing our deepest feelings and attitudes involves risk. It exposes our weaknesses and defenses. Defenses protect our ego. We can be hurt. Self-disclosure is likely to be made only to those

whom we see as trustworthy. Family and friends traditionally fulfill these roles and have likely shown their concern and care. We
are reluctant to trust and show ourselves to persons with whom
our experiences have been clouded by their negative behavior,
discriminatory practices, or both. The history of race in America
clouds the relationship every White therapist has with their Black
clients.

African American women continue this tradition of silence.
So like our foremothers, we hold in our pain. We keep our secrets. We take care of other people, even when they are kicking
our backsides. We develop fix-it mentalities that cause us to over-
work. We feel guilty about taking care of ourselves.

Tolerance for pain evolved from issues of safety and trust. It
was futile for our foremothers to talk about their pain to anyone
who could do something about it. There were no protectors, thus
they were open to danger, harm, and inhumane treatment. The
friendships formed among themselves provided nurturing and
enabled them to pass on survival skills without interference from
slave masters. *Grin and bear it,* an unspoken mandate modeled by
slave mothers, has been passed down through generations. Consequently, Black women have borne emotional and physical pain
for so long that living with it is a normal state.

To change this behavior requires us to take care of ourselves
first. (It's harder to pull someone else up when we're on our
knees.) Talking about the concerns that we feel are unspeakable
is a crucial step because the energy that holds the information inside can then be released for creative use. This also holds true
when we tell the people in our lives what we need from them

instead of assuming that they should already know. The comfort level we achieve with new behavior strengthens our emotional safety and security. We can then trust and allow into our lives those reliable people who not only care what happens to us but are also available, without penalties, when we need them.

Perhaps one reason for the wide appeal of Terry McMillan's *Waiting to Exhale* is that it taps into our vulnerability, safety, and trust issues and tolerance for pain. It reveals some of our weaknesses and strengths; our need to be loved, protected, and valued; and our will to survive.

Sexual Predators and Our Bodies

Those who enslaved our foremothers fostered images of Black women as sexually uninhibited and available to give others pleasure anytime they wanted it. Apparently, owners excused themselves from any moral code in committing the vile acts since slaves were legally property. Furthermore, such legal sanction may have allowed "Christian" men to overlook the religious taboos against sex between master and slave. At any rate, the forced sexual encounters bred feelings of unworthiness in the victims.

The negative images and women's silence about sexual, physical, and emotional abuse have lasted till this day, and we endure them. With few exceptions, our portrayals in movies and television remain stereotypes: wanton hussies, mammies, head-shaking smart-mouthed mamas, and gangster girls.

The bashing continues through music that calls us disrespectful, degrading names, ridicules us as insensitive battle-axes, and blames us for the problems of Black men. Unfortunately, there are Black men (and even women) who sing and promote these songs. When we consider the negative associations assigned to our bodies, race, and gender, it is amazing that we have any self-esteem at all. Nevertheless, our will to survive is strong. It propels us forward in different ways at different speeds and levels—often with pain.

Self-esteem—the evaluations we make and express about our personal worth—varies. Degrees of high and low self-esteem are influenced greatly by the type of support network surrounding us and the self-reflections we receive from them. Primary family groups that offer consistently positive, supportive environments and appropriate boundaries provide the nourishment that fosters higher self-esteem. The reverse is also true. Negative, unsupportive environments foster lower self-esteem. Internalized messages of unworthiness and the need for love are reasons why some women allow their bodies to be used.

Hardships have fine-tuned Black women's survival instincts. These instincts are strong because they have been developed and tested throughout the centuries. Black women have to work harder. It takes energy to counteract the negative forces directed toward us and to manage the multiple roles in which we are cast. The struggle sometimes produces depression from the pressures of our realities. Fine-tuned survival instincts, however, help to counter feelings of low self-esteem.

The greater tragedy is to society itself. When Black women are forced to operate in survival modes, our potential contributions to society are diminished. Energy is lost that could otherwise be directed in constructive, creative ways. We have only to look at the lives of Black women like Sojourner Truth, Harriet Tubman, Rosa Parks, Maya Angelou, and Whoopi Goldberg, to name a few, and the contributions they made despite adversity. Imagine the many other Black women whose potential contributions to society were lost because their creative energy was consumed simply in the act of surviving.

Practices and the use of products that enhance beauty are among the survival instincts that neutralize society's negative evaluations. Hair and hair products, personal care, and food are readily available to us for pampering ourselves. Research on Black consumer behavior reflects significant yearly increases in Black women's spending on personal care services—hair salons, manicures, and massages—and cosmetics and hair care products. We use these products as we feel the need.

These patterns can be viewed positively or negatively, depending on who does the defining. Personal services and products are acceptable tools for body care and beauty enhancement. The seemingly widespread use of hair products and cosmetics by some Black women might suggest low self-acceptance and self-esteem. It appears to send a message to young girls, for instance, that their natural hair states are not acceptable. Alternately, for other Black women, it just means time and convenience, fashion experimentation, and pampering.

Food and eating rituals can also be viewed as survival instincts in operation. Food serves many purposes in Black women's lives. It represents a form of freedom. We eat to celebrate—choosing, preparing, and eating what and when we want, despite others' opinions or the consequences of our selections. Food serves as a companion when we are lonely. It serves as a consoler when we are depressed. In times of distress, eating captures portions of the celebration theme in our community and offers solace.

The contradictions and paradoxes of enslavement produced a duality in Black women. On the one hand, our strength shows in both the will to survive hardships and in survival itself. On the other, our fear of being alone and mistrust of others lie at the bottom of the well.

Our will to survive forges us ahead. At the same time, we protect our vulnerable spots so we are not destroyed. Religious worship, prayer, and praise rituals; immediate and extended family affirmations; artistic, educational, and civic achievement; and therapy all help to counter the esteem-lowering effects from society.

Our realities—the legacies from enslavement, everyday life stressors, racism, and sexism—make Black women's lives and therapeutic experiences different from any other group. The challenge is to move beyond such legacies to enjoy fuller lives. Therapy as a partnership can help in learning to do this. Black women have been silent about adverse circumstances and treatment for too long. It is time to speak out, choose alternatives, and redefine. When this happens, we will restore and enhance our full power and experience a new freedom.

TWO

First Visits

MAY ARRIVED AT THE EXACT HOUR OF HER APPOINTMENT and answered in monosyllables as I greeted her in the waiting room. Without shedding the navy pea jacket she wore over a matching skirt and sweater, she followed closely behind me up the stairs but stopped just inside my office door. Her large brown eyes were fixed on me. With an outstretched arm, I directed May to the oversized sofa in the middle of the room and sat closest to her in one of the two adjacent cushioned, straight-back chairs. She sat rigidly on the edge of her seat looking wide-eyed at me.

"Northeast" and "old people" popped out when I asked about where she lived and her neighborhood. Seeing my quizzical look about old people, May added that it was an old neighborhood with old people. Most of the children had grown up and moved away, except a few like her.

To inquiries about schools and the one thing May most enjoyed doing, she dutifully recited the names and locations of the elementary and high schools she attended and the subjects studied. Interrupting herself, May asked if she had to lie down on the couch. I answered no, not unless she wanted to.

May proceeded without missing a beat, naming teachers and the things about them she remembered. As her one-word responses grew into sentences, she removed her jacket and inched back until she was seated comfortably. Her gaze shifted to the lit fireplace in front of the sofa. Softly and rapidly, May told me about her ability to draw.

From about age seven, when alone she doodled, moving on to drawing cartoon figures and animals, then sketches of people for entertainment. May loved to draw and paint with watercolors but confined the artworks to her room—sometimes hung on the walls but mostly kept in boxes under her bed. Her parents only saw them when they entered her space.

I waited for the rest of the story when abruptly May confessed: "I really didn't want to come to therapy. You know, I've never been to a counselor before. I thought about it a long, long time before I decided to come. I asked my cousin about it when things started to get me down too much."

"What things?"

"Why I'm stuck. Why I can't make things happen for myself." Turning from me to face the empty chair at the opposite end of the sofa, May explained, "I can tell you more if I don't look at you."

I remained quiet.

After a few seconds' pause, she continued. "For years, I've

been on the sidelines. I watched the girls who were popular. They seemed invited everywhere. Even if my parents had let me, I didn't know how to be a part of the group. I didn't know what to say or how to act. I've been miserable for a long time. I've been trying to understand why I act like I do."

May turned to me. "What can I do to change? What can I do to feel better about myself? I'm sick of all of this." She looked away again. "I'm trapped in a time warp looking at life passing by me. I'll be an old woman still living at home with my parents. I'm not doing anything; not going anywhere. I don't seem to have what it takes to be successful. I don't know how to make the right connections. It's like beating my head against a stone wall."

"What keeps you from making changes?"

"Well"—May paused while dropping her head—"my finances for one. I have to pay off my bills. Serious debt. My credit is shot. It should be easy managing my money since I only have to pay the telephone and gas bills, but it's not. Before I know it, I'm spending every penny I make."

"You're in a bind."

May nodded. "Yeah. But that's just half. I don't even know how to make the right moves. Especially when it comes to men. I thought about marriage but that's not easy either."

"How do you mean?"

"There are no men. Eligible Black men. But even if I met one, I wouldn't know whether he was for real or not. That's part one. Part two is my family and my religion. They don't like us dating outside our church but there aren't any men inside either.

The ones my age are married or already gone. I want to go outside, too."

"Have you gone outside?"

"Sort of."

"What happened?"

"Nothing. I couldn't get it together. When guys approach me, I get tongue-tied and can't think of anything interesting to say. I freeze up. Usually, I just stand there looking stupid after I say hello and how are you. I guess I'm too quiet and too boring because none of them ever come back." Her voice trailed to a whisper. May closed her eyes and bowed her head. Her sadness penetrated the room.

"Together, we'll find out what needs to be done."

May looked slowly around the room. Dark brown shoulder-length hair framed her face. Tinted lip gloss was the only trace of makeup on her flawless skin. She laid her head back to stare at the ceiling while she talked almost nonstop. Quietly, I leaned toward her to learn more about her life and the circumstances that had brought her into therapy.

MAY'S LONELINESS HAD SEVERAL DIMENSIONS. ONE WAS being without a man. The prospect of living alone deepened her fears and insecurity. Declining church membership and failure to attract young people limited the number of available males. May was caught in the middle. There were no prospects for her within the sect, but she wasn't prepared to go outside.

The loneliness of being without a man linked with May's mental messages that said she should be married and was not fulfilled unless she had a man in her life. Society reinforced these messages by subtle and bold actions toward unmarried women with and without children. Isolation—a feeling of not belonging—was another dimension of her loneliness. It set May apart to encounter life's trials and joys alone. Suppressing feelings of loneliness embarrassed and hurt her.

Thirty-two-year-old May was an only child, never married, who worked as a drafter in an architectural firm. She lived with her sixty-nine-year-old retired parents. They followed a strict religious tradition, held prominent church positions, and had reared May to accept their judgment without question. The climate in their home was pleasant and quiet, but no one talked much to each other. Compliments and other expressions of approval were rare, even for the exceptional pencil-and-ink sketches and paintings that May had produced through the years.

May's and her parents' lives centered on a small, family church of aging men and women where the norm for the few children among them was to be seen and not heard. Most of the younger population were related by birth or marriage, and social events were held at the church or at members' homes.

Their religious lifestyle did not include May's participation in school extracurricular and social activities beyond the family and church. At school she'd been quiet, compliant, and overlooked by teachers and students alike. Fading into the background dwindled her confidence and ease in socializing.

College had been disappointing to May.

It was to have been her way out—May's chance to blossom. Hope that art would distinguish her at her local college turned into more disappointment when, again, she became one in the crowd: the overlooked, quiet one just like before. Teachers disappointed her. The encouragement she expected from them did not happen. Little by little, her zeal faded. She dropped out with below-average grades after her second year of fine arts studies.

No one had helped her much in the two years at college. She had liked the modern, fully equipped studios and materials but was not prepared to be on her own. She had no friends. Classmates toiled with their own adjustment problems. The support and reassurance May craved were missing and she did not know how to get them. The absence of recognition and value for May's artistic abilities had devastated her.

During the summer after her second year, May found a job as a secretary to a group of architects and stayed until the company went out of business five years later. From there she had come to her present job seven years ago.

May moved between home, work, and church. Her cousin and only friend initiated their telephone conversations. In May's free time alone, she mostly slept and rarely sketched anymore. She indicated no health problems but reported slipped weight. Her mother warned that 110 pounds was not enough weight for her five-foot-eight-inch frame and worried that May would waste away if she didn't eat more.

★   ★   ★

Fifteen minutes of our fifty-minute first session remained. May knew the length of the session from our prior telephone conversation. She glanced at the wall clock and continued to talk. I called attention to the time remaining and invited May to tell me what she wanted to happen in therapy. I'd given her the question earlier to think about.

May looked away as she answered. "I want to come out of this shell. I want to feel more comfortable with myself." She paused about fifteen seconds after each of my probes.

"Anything else?"

"I want to be able to talk to people without stumbling all over myself." She bowed her head and pulled alternately at each hand.

"Anything else?"

May spoke almost in a whisper. "I want to get rid of this pain. I'm tired of it."

"Yes," I acknowledged softly. "It's time for it to go."

We sat quietly.

I broke the silence to explain that we would do something about all the things May mentioned. "This process restores personal power. Now, it's outside you. We'll find it and bring it back.

"Your senses are important in this process. We'll use them to think, talk, listen, laugh, cry, read, write, and try out new behavior, all confidentially. You can be yourself. I will be your support person as you identify your issues and examine them from different perspectives. You set the pace and do the work. I'll nudge you when you need it.

"Any questions about what I have told you so far?"

May listened intently and answered no.

"Tell me what you heard me say."

"I'm going down a new road but I'm not going by myself. You'll be with me while I learn the way."

"Exactly. Assignments will help. Your first one is to begin a journal."

"Do I have to write in it every day?"

"No, it's not required, but it is good to write every day for the first few days to establish a pattern of writing often."

"What should I write about?"

"About the things you think about most. Write about what bothers you. Write about our session today. We'll talk more about the journal at another time. Any questions for me?"

May shook her head to mean no.

I stood. May didn't budge but offered an additional bit of forgotten information she labeled important. I signaled for her to join me as I walked to the door and suggested that since her time was up, she take a minute to jot down the thoughts in the waiting room. She could also, I said, write about them in her journal to share at our next meeting, unless something more pressing arose. May stood reluctantly and walked to the door, where she tried again to extend the time by introducing a new topic.

Talking about her feelings and personal affairs was a new experience. The exclusive attention and acceptance were also new. May tested the time limits for her session and I soon learned that getting her to leave was a task to master.

★   ★   ★

MAY'S FIRST SESSION REMINDED ME OF OTHER BLACK women who reached out to therapy for help to relieve their distress. Many of these same women struggled not only with depression, isolation, and pain but also with negative perceptions of therapy and reservations about using it. Interacting involved them personally and directly in the therapeutic process and strengthened their commitment to it. Without commitment, they left therapy as soon as they felt better.

Feeling better is just one part of the process. Talking freely about problems that have been held inside gives relief. However, the commitment in therapy involves staying long enough to learn how to cope with both the current and future problems that will recur in our lives.

May came to find solutions and heal. I thought about how to help her commit to therapy. This is what I decided: Take away the mystery and stereotype—so I told her what to expect and periodically explained what I was doing and why. Create ownership—we discussed what she wanted from therapy and how she could make it happen. Weaken the perception of therapy as a place for crazy people—I relaxed and related to her as a friend.

MAY ENTERED THE NEXT SESSION CLENCHING HER JOURnal. Daily entries written late into the night had captured feelings released in last week's session. Again, she sat on the edge of her seat but answered immediately when I asked about them.

"What stood out in your writing?"

"I think, my sadness." Staring past me, she paused. "My anger."

"Anger?"

Tears formed and trickled as May spoke. "Nothing goes right for me. Like my job. I have good work habits and know I'm good at it but I still get overlooked for promotions because I don't speak up. My bosses know I do good work but they take me for granted. Other people come in and move ahead of me just like everywhere else. I don't get any breaks."

"You're hurt."

"Yeah." May's voice faded. "I'm getting to where I don't care anymore. I don't want to be this way but I'm tired of everybody. I'm tired of crying. I've been crying a lot lately."

"What's happening on the job now?"

"They brought in a White girl at a higher salary than mine and expect me to train her. She's the same age as me and she's not as qualified as me. She doesn't even have as much experience as I have."

"What have you done about it?"

"Nothing. I don't know what to do."

"Who have you talked with about the situation?"

"Nobody."

"Who do you expect to read your mind?"

"They ought to know."

"Oh?"

"They *ought* to know." May swept the back of her hand across her tears.

"Ought has no power, May. What options do you have?" I

paused before continuing. "Look at your options. Think about the possible actions you can take. Write about them in your journal. We'll discuss them in here."

May's isolation and unfamiliarity with options fostered her helplessness and frustration. Knowledge of them would strengthen her. I reminded May that something could be done about anything. It was a matter of finding what needed to be done and the right person to do it, whether that was her or someone else.

In our sessions, it was important to restore May's sense of personal worth and power to control her life. She needed to understand her authority to choose actions that would make her life better. When she allowed other people to choose for her routinely, she gave them her power.

"What do you want to happen on the job? Do you know what you want?" I asked.

"I want some respect. I want them to recognize that I do a good job." May exhaled. "I want bonuses for my good work, like everyone else. I want to know about opportunities to advance and how to advance. I'm tired of being overlooked. I've been ignored all my life."

"What have you learned from being overlooked?"

"I never thought about it." May folded her arms across her chest and said nothing for several moments. "I can't assume people will do right by me. They'll do what I let them do to me. I have to let them know what I want from them."

"True. Where can you apply the lessons?"

She paused again after each response. "My job. Men. My

social life. Uh, finances. My future. Uh, men. I don't know. I need to think about it some more."

"Look at the ways you give away your power and allow others to control you."

"I can do that?"

"Yes. If you want to."

May was accustomed to being told what to do. Generating alternatives offered new behavior to stimulate her thinking and feeling on her authority to make changes. My probes tapped into her attempt at change.

After several years of working, May had pursued what she imagined was an appealing image. But her new sports car, stylish clothes, miscellaneous purchases, and weekly hair and nail treatments had plunged her into debt and locked her into living at home—temporarily, she thought. May looked good but her pain remained because the changes were cosmetic. Frustration drove her deeper into her shell. Regular contact with her cousin in church-related activities was her only outlet since she no longer drew.

May had always listened intently as her cousin talked about problems and experiences. She also noted gradual changes in her attitude and behavior. When May had later questioned them, her cousin had told about her experience in therapy with me two years earlier and how it helped. May mulled over the information for several months before deciding to try it.

"Any more lessons?"

"I have to know what I want for myself. Take care of myself. That's new."

"Yes. What does taking care of yourself mean to you, right now?"

"I guess, getting rid of stuff I've been hanging on to. Stop being so unsure about everything."

"Good guesses. Clean stuff out. What happens when you leave food in the refrigerator for a long time?"

"It gets moldy."

"What happens when you let it stay there longer?"

"It gets rotten and smelly."

"And contaminates everything in the box, if it's left long enough. We're cleaning stuff out."

May glanced at the clock when she heard my summary statements but adjusted her body in the seat as if she'd just arrived. We acknowledged our mutual comfort level and contracted for ten additional weekly sessions to work on her goals. At the end of that period, we would evaluate our time together and decide on next steps. The short initial contract period created an expectation that the work to be done in therapy could be achieved. It also eased both May's resistance to the process and her fear of being viewed as a "mental sickie."

Like clockwork, May began another theme from her journal and, again, I interrupted to explain that exceeding the fifty-minute limit imposed on the time allotted to the next person, and ended the session. May joined me at the door and followed my outstretched arm out of the room as we said good-bye.

It occurred to me that African American folkways had influenced May's expectation of time in therapy. Our therapeutic relationship resembled a close friendship in which she shared the most intimate details of her life with me. Since similar relationships rarely imposed time limits, I understood May's difficulty in letting go in therapy. Perhaps that was also my own unconscious motivation when I called her after her first visits—to extend the warmth of the sessions.

IN OUR NEXT TWO SESSIONS, MAY LOOKED DIRECTLY AT me and talked without prompting. We focused on the immediate issues at her job. Her completed homework assignment identified several courses of action. For each, she examined the strengths, weaknesses, benefits, and drawbacks. May introduced them by reading from her journal:

> I'm going for broke. I'm sick of this. They'll give me a raise or they'll fire me. So what. If I stay like it is now, they'll treat me like a dog for real. They're cold. It's humiliating. I don't have but one performance review. One in five years. Shoot. I ain't taking this no more. Shoot. I'll get something to tide me over until I can do better. Shoot. McDonald's always got openings. I'll go there if I have to. I got a roof over my head. Oh, thank God Mom and Dad don't mind me living at home. I'm gonna get this together.
>
> I can stay on this J-O-B but that's no change, I just have to grin and bear it. But that's what I always do. Good old May. Just tolerate anything. Is that good enough anymore? No. It's too painful.
>
> Talk to the manager. Yeah, right. I can hear him now: "You

never complained. I took that to mean you were satisfied." Yeah, right. It's time to discuss my performance and ask for recognition. I know I've done good work but I'll bet he'll try to find some way to twist it around. Anyhow, he can agree with me, disagree, or fire me outright. Couldn't be any worse than it is now.

May continued to discuss the options she pondered. She would search the job market and transfer her skills to a similar job or quit to return to school. Staying at home eliminated big living expenses. Loans and grants to pay for school and part-time employment to pay off her bills offered further possibilities. This time, she intended to be clear about her goals for school. May answered my question about next steps when she announced her plan to get more information about each alternative and choose the best ones.

Problem solving permitted May to apply the technique to situations where she needed clarity and direction. She understood *trapped* meant no way out, but *free* meant to both generate and evaluate options then choose and act on them. Examining the courses of action helped her to plan effective steps of action. I encouraged May to use this process until it became automatic.

Initially, May looked for signs of approval on her approach to her problems. The supportive environment, however, bolstered her confidence and helped her to realize she did not need my approval on decisions about her life. Though desirable, my affirmation was no longer necessary.

★   ★   ★

AT THE END OF EACH SUCCEEDING SESSION, MY SUMMARY probes summoned May's descriptions of meaningful activity, her feelings as she engaged in it, and activity that helped and hindered her progress. Her responses helped us both to evaluate our time together. May recognized her responses as closing statements and peeped at the clock. We reviewed her homework assignments to take action steps for work and to identify other situations where she could apply her learning.

May did not start new topics at the end of our continuing sessions but did not move either. At one, I repeated the exit ritual. At the next, I remained seated, looked at her, and announced, "It's time to G-O." At most of the remaining sessions, we took turns standing first and trailing each other to the door.

May applied the problem-solving process to self-assessment. She inventoried her knowledge, skills, abilities, and job accomplishments to develop a résumé. Her job description and a performance guideline prepared May for a meeting with her manager. More confidence and clarity about what she wanted helped her to follow through.

Comfortable with her sessions, May always appeared on time in casual wool skirt suits, journal clenched and Coach bag slung over her shoulders.

One day she hesitated. I wondered what was going on with her but waited and watched as she slid to the edge of her seat and back. After several starts, she mentioned her parents. Reluctance to talk about them stalled her. I reassured May that she could safely talk about anything. On my saying the sun wouldn't stop shining and the sky wouldn't fall when she did, May laughed out loud and sat back. After a long silent moment followed by a deep sigh, she shared.

"I know my parents love me. I know they mean well but our contacts are so limited, I'm not prepared to deal with people outside our little circle. I can hardly deal with those inside it. My parents try to protect me from everything. I appreciate everything they do. I really do."

I listened as May scooted to the edge of her seat and spoke in a slightly raised, staccato voice. "Why did they keep to themselves so much? Why didn't they expose me to more people? They could have supervised it. Why am I an only child?"

"You're angry."

"Yeah, and I feel bad about it." May dropped her head. "I'm not supposed to be angry with my parents. They support me. They love me. They're good people. I will do anything for my parents. They're *good* people."

"Who are you trying to convince?"

"They are good but I have to admit, I feel cheated. I am angry. And I'm disappointed with my life. Every time I think this I feel terrible. Every time I say this out loud, I feel worse."

The acknowledged anger at her parents heightened May's guilt. Some of the guilt came from inbred messages that told her anger was bad, ungrateful, and would be punished. May's anger also came from disappointment. Interpretations from religious teaching led her to expect rewards for being good, but it didn't happen as she had imagined. Life had not given her what she wanted.

"You have to blame somebody," May charged. "It's confusing.

You're brought up to believe, and pray, and all that. And you try to do what's right. And you think that things are going to turn out like you want."

"Talking about God?"

"Y-yes. We can talk about God?"

"Yes."

"But you're not supposed to."

"Who said so?"

"Oh—uh, nobody. I just assumed. That's something else to think about. I need to write about this." May abandoned the topic.

The subject of God threatened May. I let it go, knowing that she would consider the issue in her own time. She introduced a lighter subject by telling me about her upcoming high school class reunion. She had never attended before and spent the remainder of the session talking about it. When I told her that our time was almost up, she sprang another question.

"What about the journal? You said you were going to tell me more about the journal."

"Sure. The journal serves three purposes. It's a way to unpack your feelings."

"Like I'm learning to do now."

"Yes. Releasing them frees your inner space so you can use it more creatively. Remember the refrigerator. There's more room outside than there is inside."

"I like that."

"Me too. The journal provides a reference point to see your growth. There will be noticeable differences in your attitude and behavior to which people around you will see and respond. You can't change other people but you can change their responses to you. I guarantee it. The journal also binds the time between our visits."

"Write, talk, listen, laugh, cry, read, think, and try out new behavior confidentially. See, I heard you."

We laughed. I liked May. She sensed it and looked constantly for ways to extend her time in therapy. While I was firm in getting her out, I recognized that our relationship provided a model for her to learn to interact more effectively with others.

MAY BEGAN HER NEXT SESSION BY TELLING HOW SHE WRESTLED with guilt feelings during the past week. She read excerpts about it from her journal:

> So much is going on in my head. Sometimes I think I'm a disappointment because I haven't branched out from home. Seems like I ought to be doing more but they don't say anything. We need to talk. Maybe I can understand if I can ask them about things. I've got questions.
>
> Dr. S. must be off her own rocker. Question God? Naw, naw; that's not right. You don't question God. Because, she'll say, because? Because I'm afraid to. Something might happen to me if I do. That's why.

I commented, "Guilty and scared."

"Yeah."

I abandoned the subject of God when I saw May's eyes widen and body stiffen.

"You say you ought to be doing more?"

"I told you I feel like I'm in a time warp. Stuck is what it is. Stuck. I ought to be doing more to make them proud of me."

"What makes you think they aren't?"

"I'm still living at home and practically broke."

"So?"

"So it's not supposed to happen that way. That's not the way the story's supposed to be."

"Oh?"

"I thought things would be different for me. I keep trying. Sometimes I wonder if I'm doomed. Or cursed. Maybe I'm not supposed to make it. I don't know. I guess I'm not proud of my-self. Thinking about it wears me out."

"I guess so. That's a lot to carry around. What are you going to do about it?"

"I don't know, yet. Try to understand."

MAY STRUGGLED WITH STRONG EMOTIONS—DISAPPOINTMENT, fear, and guilt—but the guilt was especially difficult and painful for her. It carried elements of disappointment, fear of punishment, shame, regret, and feelings of low self-worth. Guilt—the feeling of wrongness—occurred under different circumstances and in-vaded all aspects of her life. Like many of us, May felt guilty when she did something wrong, thought she did something wrong, or when comments or actions of others stirred guilt in her. All came from messages on her mental tapes.

May punished herself with guilt by using *ought-to* and *should-have* messages. They were like heavy invisible bags at each end of a rope wrapped around her neck—one filled with *ought-to* resting on her chest and the other filled with *should-have* on her back. May set the bags into motion for self-beatings each time she lamented what should or ought to have been. The weight and pounding wore heavy on her. She faced dragging the bags every-where or putting them in the trash where they belonged. To move ahead, she had to be free of them.

Family lifestyle and parental control permitted little freedom to establish an independent adult identity. Since May neither questioned nor expressed how she felt, her parents did not know how deeply she hurt. May longed for a different relationship with them—one in which she could talk more openly and ques-tion them about their life, religion, and practices.

The *accept-without-question* message on May's mental tape fueled anger and guilt. More probes into her family life expanded our search for answers. She didn't know a lot about her parents. Both were quiet. Most questions received scant replies from her mother. When May asked once about her mother's loneliness and isolation growing up, the answer was *there is nothing to tell* and the subject was closed. Imagining that she would have fared better if her mother had talked more, anger rose each time May thought of her backwardness and isolation. She felt rejected, desperate, alone, and unlovable.

★   ★   ★

My suggestion at one session that her mother join us prompted an agitated response before I even completed the statement. May didn't think it was a good idea, citing the funny ideas some people held about a person seeing a therapist: They think something is wrong or the person is crazy and people talk. May didn't want it known to anyone that she was in therapy, not even her mother.

Sinking into her seat, May continued to explain. Her tightly knit church group wouldn't keep such a secret. Telling her mother would be telling her father, uncles, and aunts. Before long, they would stretch May before the altar to pray for her deliverance. She dreaded the attention her therapy visits would bring and the association of *therapy* with *crazy*.

May's attitude also shed light on the relationship with her mother, but May wasn't ready to look further at it this day. She declared that since therapy had worked for her cousin, similar changes would satisfy her. The finality in her voice suggested she wanted therapy without family involvement. May stared out the window as we waited in silence. After a long minute and a half she acknowledged her pain. I asked her to tell me more about it.

May shrugged her shoulders then folded her arms tightly in front of her. "I hurt inside all the time. My pain is constant. It's active. Mostly around my heart but my stomach, too. Sometimes I feel I don't have a bottom in my stomach. It's an empty, sinking feeling. And my heart; my heart feels like a pair of hands is trying to pull it out of my chest. Sometimes the pain is quiet but most of the time it's not. It throbs. Aches. 'Specially when I'm lonely and isolated. The pain is intense. It's hard to talk about. I've kept it inside so long.

"I have my questions about things. Why me? I feel bad when I want something different. My mind keeps saying, *Appreciate the good parts of life and be satisfied.* I know. And I feel shame. And I get scared because I feel like I'm being punished for not appreciating things. I know I've got to deal with my disappointments and my anger. I see that now."

"How do you feel talking about it?"

"Raw. Scared. My heart is beating fast. Unprotected. A little relieved."

"Say more."

"I feel scared and shaky like I'm naked and people are standing around looking at me. It's not a good feeling. Not a good feeling at all. I keep thinking, *Why me?* I never bothered anybody. I never hurt anybody."

"Yes. It does seem unfair."

"But at least I've said it out loud. I've never done that before."

"It's a good start. Continue by writing in your journal. Pain is backed-up energy with no release. It feeds on itself and signals that something needs attention. Pain won't go away until you attend to it."

For homework, I recommended Psalm Twenty-three, found in the Old Testament of the Holy Bible or from a book of the Psalms. After she read it, she should answer the questions:

- What is this psalm asking of me?

- What is it saying to me?

- How does it apply to my pain and life today?

The exercise offers comfort during painful and difficult times.

I thanked May for sharing and expressed appreciation for her openness. May stood, offered me her hand, hesitated for a split second, then hugged me. Surprised at not crying while talking about her pain, May reasoned she had shed all of her tears. She found the assignment interesting and planned to complete it.

AT THE FOLLOWING SESSION MAY PREPARED TO READ FROM her journal. Instead, I asked her to just talk about the most meaningful events from her reflections and writing. Unasked questions piled inside and smothered her, she told me. Finding the courage to make changes in her life unsettled her. I asked for more on the message and expectations around her guilty feelings, her disappointments, loneliness, and esteem.

More guilt related to anger at her parents. She blamed them for inadequate preparation to function in the larger world and lamented because she blamed them. She was mad at God. He disappointed her, too. She felt overlooked by him. May had run from this topic before. Now I reintroduced it.

"What did you overlook from God?" May questioned what I meant as she looked at me and away. "Opportunities that were open to you?" I pressed.

She jerked her head toward me and exclaimed, "What?"

After a short silence to let the question linger, I repeated, "Opportunities that were open to you."

Her words popped out. "What opportunities?"

"Perhaps you need to take the question with you and find some answers. You may see something that you haven't seen before."

No response from May.

"Talk about how you're feeling right now."

"My stomach's churning. My head is hot and feels like it's getting bigger."

"What's the emotion?"

"Anger."

"Say some more about it."

"It's the same feeling I have when I want to protest. But I don't say anything. I guess that's why people feel they can overlook me. I never show anything. I never say anything."

"You have a lot to think about. Anger is a legitimate emotion. The danger is in what we do with it. We'll continue to look at ways to manage anger. And guilt."

OVER SEVERAL SESSIONS, MAY CONSIDERED BOTH. WE examined how guilt surfaced at any time, particularly with unresolved issues; how *take-care-of-others* messages summoned guilt; and how it played through *I-am-selfish-to-put-myself-first* and *I-am-self-centered-if-I-take-care-of-myself* messages until erased or replaced. Guilt abounded when May did for herself and when she could not fulfill the expectations of others. At other times, personal purchases or taking time for herself evoked guilt, as if she were cheating. The tension from guilt and anger became a companion and accepted as an expected part of life.

Shifts from patterns learned in childhood often awakens guilt—in all of us. Tasks performed by May's mother provided pictures of how things were done. May retained them and mimicked the behavior because it was what she knew how to do. Her mother, like many of ours, did not always fill in the missing explanations of why she did certain things in certain ways—perhaps for protection or from resistance. Nonetheless, attempts to reject or abandon known patterns without understanding them arouses guilt. The resulting guilt prevents decision making that produces the results we want. May learned differently in therapy.

In the sessions that followed, May returned to job concerns. Continuing her self-examination, she looked carefully at behavior that permitted others to take her for granted. May rarely expressed concerns and responded often to unreasonable requests. Her timidity allowed people to violate her basic human rights.

Personal assessment forced her to identify positive self-aspects. This awareness and emphasis gradually weakened May's focus on and instant recall of her faults and spawned a better self-view. May added assertive responses and addressed matters that concerned her. She learned to say no and to look for new ways to manage old situations.

Reassured that her new responses did not require negative, aggressive behavior but offered opportunities for others to choose from the information she provided, May worked harder. She practiced sharing with others the effect of their behavior on her along with suggestions to them on how to improve the situation. She understood that the information might or might not be used. When her feedback was ignored, May clearly knew her options were to accept the situation as it stood or to choose a more satisfying one. The process simply required clarity about the issues and choice, not fighting.

As an initial action step, May arranged a work review with her manager. From her job description, she discussed her defined responsibilities and duties, highlighting the ways she met and exceeded the requirements. May also addressed the demeaning messages sent to her when the company had paid a higher salary to the new White female employee with fewer qualifications and less experience. May's growing confidence allowed her not only to meet with the manager but also to accept firing as a possible consequence.

WE HAD REACHED THE MOMENT OF EVALUATING MAY'S progress toward the goals we'd established at the beginning of our agreement. Before we began, she shared excitement at following through on the meeting with her manager. Nothing spectacular had happened. He listened mostly with no expression. May had pressed forward, despite the tightness in her chest and sweaty palms. Thorough preparation eased the anxiety somewhat. The written materials, anticipated questions, rehearsals of the information to gain poise, and willingness to both accept the worst possible consequence and conquer her fear about it all helped May to present her concerns.

In meeting with her manager, May achieved the goal of speaking up. Preparation and sound choices improved her effectiveness. May decided to stay on the job while she considered other career options and evaluated a return to school. Other fulfilled goals yielded additional benefits. She assigned value to herself, recognized her interests and desires as legitimate, and acted for herself in ways that built confidence and self-esteem. Better communication with her parents and clearer personal definitions remained unfinished. We contracted for ten additional sessions.

OVER THE NEXT FIVE SESSIONS, MAY WORKED THROUGH feelings about herself, family, and relationships, releasing them from the years of stored silence. Buried emotions put May in touch with her pain. In exploring their emotional content, she identified important connections that influenced her behavior.

Socialization shaped the way May acted. Her family had provided the primary contact and influence in her earliest years. From them, she acquired values and tradition. Parental control in May's life fulfilled their legal and moral responsibility to guide her movement from childhood to adulthood.

Child-rearing practices along with positive and negative events in our past leave lasting impressions on us. They influence our behavior. Identifying and examining these events help us to understand both their meaning and why they make us anxious. The connections are necessary to resolve our issues.

Understanding the connections equips us to ease the anxiety that resurfaces when we face similar situations. It gives us information to generate alternatives: that is, to either formulate new responses and try out new behavior or hold on to old ways of responding. Choosing new behavior begins the process of returning our personal power to us. Choosing not to change keeps us immobilized and stagnant.

May's parents reared her to show deference to authority. However, only her church rewarded the attitude. The people at school and work perceived the quality as weakness and received it with indifference. The difference made it easy to overlook May. She wondered if achieving her adult life changes required abandonment of family values and traditions.

May sought the answer by examining the implications of moving beyond her present social boundary. She identified her most important needs and wants, then weighed the extent she would compromise each, if any. May adopted action planning and stress management into her lifestyle. She established personal, social, and career goals, and for each, defined objectives and action steps to carry them out. May recognized the need to continue the process beyond therapy.

In ensuing weeks, May focused on independence, social skills, and money management to continue improving her competence and confidence. She reviewed the new responses to use in each defined area and applied them. With problem areas, May identified the smallest possible step to take, rehearsed how to carry it out, and acted on it between sessions.

An adult relationship with her parents remained important. They noted May's growing confidence when she began to talk openly about her thoughts and feelings. She was finally able to approach them to discuss their religion and the social limitations it placed on her. Both shared their concern about her withdrawal but were unsure of the actions to take. The lack of growth in their sect had disappointed them, too. With dismay, they watched the younger members rebel and leave, threatening the survival of the tradition and reducing May's prospects for marriage within the faith.

May's parents had themselves developed in a different environment. Their parents arranged everything, including marriage, and religious beliefs dictated their strict, nonnegotiable standards. May's parents had in turn applied these same standards. It was what they knew how to do. Nevertheless, May's parents understood the change in times and wanted her to be happy. They agreed to support her efforts as long as they remained positive.

With support from therapy, openness and talking strengthened May's relationship with her parents. She transferred the techniques to other situations and saw that changes in her behavior prompted changes in responses to her. The knowledge increased her self-esteem.

Throughout therapy, May used the homework assignments and exercises to move in the directions she defined. They included daily self-affirmations, selected reading, and resources to manage her finances and debt. She saved a small amount and contributed to household expenses. To build social and civic contacts outside her religious community, May joined an African American women's support group. I commended her actions as mature and responsible.

May's changes were not drastic but they were satisfying. The significant role church activity played in her life continued. She made friends in her support group and, when asked, told them about her religious beliefs and practices.

Recognizing marriage as only one option represented an important insight for May. It revised the expectation that she find a husband and highlighted the importance of appreciating herself with or without a man. Self-worth and self-respect promoted the creative use of her time and talents. May released herself from the pressure to achieve society's definition of the ideal family and started to live in her present reality by generating options that made her happy. As May defined and acted on what she wanted, she directed her life and minimized disappointments. Only she could do it.

Sadness, losses of interest, energy, or concentration, morbid thoughts, guilt, and feelings of unworthiness are psychological symptoms of depression. Losses of appetite or sex drive, sleep disturbances (too much or too little sleep), slow body movements, constipation, headaches, backaches, and face and neck pains are physical symptoms. May experienced a prevalent, less severe type of depression called dysthymia. The long-term, chronic symptoms of dysthymia do not disable, but they had prevented May from functioning at her best.

At one time or another, we have all felt depressed or anxious over disappointments, losses, uncertainties, or fears in our human experience. However, when three or more symptoms intensify and continue over long periods, they need attention. Depression can be treated with medication, psychotherapy, or a combination of both. Therapy alone worked for May. She participated fully and learned more effective ways to deal with her problems.

SIX MONTHS OUT OF THERAPY, MAY RETURNED THE follow-up evaluation form that I sent her to assess her therapeutic experience.

Included were the questions: What was therapy/counseling like? Did it help you? What did you learn about the therapeutic process? What did you learn about yourself? How have you applied what you have learned? In what way did your behavior change? What change did other people notice in you? Would you recommend therapy/counseling to someone else? If yes, please explain why. If no, please explain why not.

Here are May's responses:

Therapy sessions dealt with various events that occurred in my life. It dealt with my issues on male and female relationships, religion, and family history. It helped me.

I realized that there are different ways to view things. Issues or events that are viewed by one are viewed differently in the eyes of another. In my case, assuming someone is watching me or talking negatively about me was, in actuality, my imagination caused by lack of communication. Being able to communicate with others without assuming their thoughts prevents these ideas.

I learned that even though I do not talk to many people, certain topics such as my job or art, I find no problem explaining in detail. It helped me loosen up.

I have applied what I learned to making conversation at home and with people at work, church, and other places. I'm more comfortable with myself. I have returned to school, part-time, but now I have a good adviser whom I talk to and who helped me to plan my studies in fine arts. I'll finish this time.

By communicating more with people, my attitude changed. I am able to understand and know what people think, instead of assuming. A sense of relief and happiness seems to replace the anxiety and fear that was with me before.

The changes that people see in me: They seem to see a more talkative and relaxed person. My parents do. They like it. I still live at home and I have the same job but they are giving me time off when I need it for my classes. I asked for it.

I would recommend therapy to anyone who needs it because it helps to view things or events in a different way. It helps a person to understand why things happen and how to do something about them.

— MAY

THREE

They Fired Me

I LISTENED INTENTLY WITHOUT COMMENT AS VICTORIA spent a third of her first session explaining why she should not be in therapy. For a while, she stood, walked to and from the window, then sat with folded arms and X-ray eyes aimed at me as she spoke. Victoria didn't see the need for professional help. She was depressed, not crazy. Therapy never occurred as an option before her physician had suggested a talk with a therapist after he'd found no physical basis for her complaints.

Still not convinced that therapy would be useful, she promised to try it at the urging of a trusted and respected female friend. Victoria's sad facial expression, preoccupied thought, and gradual changes in behavior over the past two years had worried her friend, but she didn't know how to help.

Victoria's resistance was strong. I sensed that some of it came from the stigma of therapy; the rest from her reluctance to disclose her thoughts to me. To move us along, I suggested that we use the time to get acquainted and see if we fit comfortably enough to continue. I added that there was no pressure to return if she decided against it after our meeting.

During a brief silence Victoria's tensed shoulders relaxed slightly as she continued to stare at me. I asked what she would want me to know if this were the only opportunity ever to talk to me in my professional capacity. She named work and told me about her background and work history.

Fifty-three-year-old Victoria was an accountant with the federal government and the only African American at level GS-15 in her department. The other Black males and females were concentrated at the GS-4 through GS-6 levels, with a few scattered in grades above and below. Victoria entered federal service as a grade-three clerk-typist after high school graduation and worked for a year before entering a local college at night.

Over the next seven years, with financial assistance and released time from the government-sponsored Stay-in-School Program, Victoria earned her degree. She reached GS-15 after twenty-seven years of movement through various government agencies. Diligence and hard work, traits she'd learned at home, helped her to move ahead.

Work was not a stranger in Victoria's family. Her parents had toiled to provide a spacious, comfortable home for their nine children and dutifully held them accountable for their behavior, household tasks, and homework. As the third child and oldest daughter, Victoria had helped to care for her younger siblings. All five brothers and three sisters finished high school, as did her parents. Only Victoria attended college.

She lived at home for five years after graduation, then married. Three boys—two years apart—were born to the union but the marriage ended in divorce after eight years. Her children, now adults, lived on their own.

Gradually, she relaxed as the minutes slipped by. Near the end of the session, Victoria fell silent. Her eyes glistened and, in a quick moment, she tossed her head back to prevent tears from falling. Silence filled the room until she regained her composure. I offered my availability for follow-up and asked for permission to call her during the week. It wasn't appropriate to explain the therapeutic process because Victoria had not made a commitment and didn't need to hear about it at this point. Experiencing my support was more important because clearly she was distressed.

Before the week was out, Victoria called voluntarily for another appointment. I heard the thuds of her heels before she reached the office door. She muttered greetings, plopped onto the sofa, and shifted her large frame. Words spilled out.

"Lately, everyone has been asking me if something is wrong, that I don't seem to be myself. I know that I'm tired all the time but I didn't know it showed that much. I've put on some weight from eating too late when I can't sleep. I used to exercise at least three times a week but I don't have the desire or energy to do it anymore. It's getting to be a struggle to do anything. Sometimes, late at night I just cry. I can't seem to stop crying.

"Kris, my best friend, thought I needed to talk to a professional. We prayed together and it helped but I still couldn't quite pull myself out of this low-grade awful feeling I have. To tell the truth—I haven't even told Kris this—at times, things seem so hopeless and I feel so beaten down that I think I'd be better off dead. I wouldn't kill myself but I don't seem to care anymore. I can hardly believe I'm feeling this way.

"I used to get upset with people who said they were depressed. They would get on my nerves. I dismissed it as a passing fancy. I thought, *Sure, we all feel down at times and say we're depressed but we get over it, snap out of it.* I'm beginning to understand that depression is severe. People don't understand that it is a serious condition. I didn't."

Once Victoria started to talk, she couldn't stop. "I know why Kris was so upset. One weekend I felt so bad, I stayed in bed the whole three days. I didn't comb my hair; I didn't bathe; I didn't eat; I didn't pay my bills. I couldn't pull myself out of it." Unshed tears gleamed in her eyes.

"What's happening on the job, Victoria?" I asked.

A muscle tensed in her jaw as she sat erectly and thrust her head forward as if protecting her dignity. "They fired me!"

THINGS HAD NEVER COME EASY TO VICTORIA. SHE FOUGHT for every opportunity and seemed always to pay an extra price for it. *Personable* is not a term to describe her. In fact, Victoria's direct manner, rare smiles, and slightly raised voice when emphasizing points earned her the label *difficult.* She didn't agree with the assessment. *Realist* is the term she preferred.

Victoria had never been able to move above the GS-15 level. The changes in treatment and evaluations by her managers escalated after she'd applied for a Senior Executive Service (SES) position in upper management. Out-of-state assignments increased and were given to her without notice or briefings. She scrambled to gather the information to participate in the projects. Upon her return, the managers rated her performance as if they had provided the support that normally accompanied such assignments.

This pattern was continuous. Moreover, management monitored Victoria's arrivals and departures closely and confronted her with one- and two-minute discrepancies, even though she was known for punctuality and had arrived at work thirty to forty minutes early throughout her career.

Unsatisfactory ratings, constant needling by her manager, and shunning by her peers proved to be too stressful. While questioning her treatment at a manager-initiated confrontation, she exploded, telling her manager where to go and what to do when she got there. The manager took the behavior as a threat and summoned security guards to usher Victoria out of the building. Later, they barred her from the building.

Victoria appealed to the Merit Protection Board. She had no confidence in the Equal Employment Opportunity (EEO) office, stating that they took too long and appeared rarely to resolve the complaints routinely filed with them. She judged the process ineffective and questioned the EEO officer's authority to enforce the procedures. His low GS grade level and staff position placed them both under the same agency managers.

Clearly, two areas needed immediate attention: Victoria's depression and resource people and places to help her. We verified our mutual comfort levels and her desire to continue, then proceeded. After explaining the process, I asked for a commitment of eight sessions to work toward established goals. The commitment also included an evaluation of progress at the end of the eighth visit to determine the next steps.

Her symptoms indicated depression. As we talked about it, I mentioned that the research-supported combination of antidepressants and therapy has been confirmed as an effective treatment, especially when symptoms impair a person's ability to function effectively. I explained, also, that antidepressants are one of a class of psychotropic medications developed to control and resolve mood, affect, and behavioral problems—such as eating and sleeping. Prescribed by a physician, they relieve some of the depression while the person works through its causes in therapy.

Victoria bristled when asked to consider a medical evaluation for an antidepressant to stabilize her mood. She declined the offer, proclaiming her long-standing ability to handle her own problems and reluctance to become dependent on drugs, which to her only weak people used. I didn't belabor the point, just asked her not to completely dismiss the suggestion.

For homework, Victoria began a journal, at my urging, for several reasons: (1) to ventilate her feelings and clarify her concerns; (2) to provide a perspective from which to view her growth; and (3) to bind the time between our visits. Her first task was to identify as many support people and places as possible to help her employment situation: family, friends, attorneys, elected officials, and organizations, including those for federal personnel management and civil liberties protection. She could remove from the list, as needed.

ALTHOUGH VICTORIA FELT RELIEVED AFTER EACH SESSION, her depressive symptoms persisted. We agreed to talk briefly each day for support until her next appointment with me. Once when we met, she shared an extensive annotated list of resources. From it, she found a skilled and experienced labor relations attorney who directed the additional steps she needed to take. Before ending the session, Victoria said she didn't feel as alone and cried less but sleeplessness and anxiety still plagued her. I gave her a pamphlet on depression and encouraged her to continue writing in her journal. The writing would provide a release for the emotions she had stored for too long.

Victoria called during the week to let me know of her appointment for medication evaluation. With prompting, she wrote down questions about psychotropic medications to discuss with the doctor. Later, she would find general information on them from the Internet, books on prescription drugs, or detailed information in the *Physician's Desk Reference* at the public library or bookstores. In our session two weeks hence, Victoria reported surprise at feeling better instead of feeling drugged after taking the antidepressant. She always considered the use of psychotropic medication not only as a sign of personal weakness, but also a violation of nutritional and health practices. She still considered it a stopgap measure until her crises were resolved.

We looked at ways to handle her stress and anger. The stress management plan I suggested included physical, mental, and spiritual aspects of self-care. The anger management plan included redirecting anger energy into suitable expressions and outlets—singing, exercise, painting, or going into a room alone and shouting at the top of her voice until the immediate energy surge drained out. For now, she selected exercise and shouting.

Further probes into Victoria's support persons revealed her refusal to tell family members about her trouble because she was the support person for everyone else and didn't want them to worry. She mimicked: " 'Victoria will do it; Victoria will solve it.' "

"Why haven't you told them?"

Victoria snapped, "I told you." She emphasized each word. "I am the person who holds up everyone else."

"Why haven't you told them?" I pushed.

Fingers locked at the back of her head, Victoria stared blankly at me in thought. Moments passed in silence. With hands returned to her lap, she rubbed her fingertips together in frustration and bit her lips. "I'm ashamed. It's embarrassing. I'm supposed to know how to fix things."

I sighed, "Yeah."

"I know it doesn't make sense. You know, it's been hard trying to make a way in this work world. I've been through some real hell. I got real tired of fighting for right. Why does everything have to be explained to them? I had to always try to make sure that we were included. A lot of times, the deals were done and the contracts signed before I even heard about them. It was a constant source of irritation."

Victoria shook her head. "You would think that after twenty-seven years, I could finish my career and ease out comfortably like they do. Huh!

"It irks me to remember how long I had to stay in the same grade with outstanding evaluations and have the White ones sail past me. You can't imagine the number of ignorant-newcomer ninnies I trained, only to have them promoted ahead of me. But I prevailed. I was intent on it. I figured the experience would break me or make me strong. This last move is a blip—a terrible blow—but I'll make it. I'll just keep drawing on my two mainstays, Psalm Twenty-seven and Maya Angelou's poems, 'And Still I Rise' and 'Phenomenal Woman.' They've seen me through a lot."

We refocused on family to help Victoria work through the issues preventing her from asking for support and confronted the assumptions underlying her decisions.

"So you are ashamed to ask your family for help. What is the worst possible thing that can happen if you ask?"

Victoria stared at me a while before speaking. "They can say no or they could ignore me." She paused again. "They could be disappointed in me or scared."

"Scared?"

"Scared that I will no longer be there for them. Be there to provide for them."

"Who's scared?"

Victoria didn't answer. I waited.

"Me, I guess." Her voice trailed.

"Say more."

"It scares me to think that I might be out of control and can't keep things going. Everyone has always depended on me. Asked me. Relied on me."

"What is the best possible thing that can happen if you ask?"

"They can say yes and be there for me?"

"Question or answer?"

"Answer. They can say yes and be there for me."

"What keeps you from focusing on a positive response from them?"

"My pride, I guess. I've always been self-reliant."

"That's okay, but now you need help. There is a scriptural passage in the fourth chapter of James that says you have not because you ask not. How does the statement apply to you?"

Victoria answered quickly. "It makes me feel too vulnerable."

"That's all right. It's new behavior. Is there anything that leads you to believe that your family will not support you?"

"Not really."

"Well, it's time to collect your chips. Ask for help. If it is there, fine. If not, we'll look somewhere else for help and support."

We also probed and questioned the notion that she had to be a superwoman.

- How did she know to be a superwoman?

- From where did the idea come?

- Why does she feel the need to sustain the superwoman image?

- What needs to happen to change this notion?

- How often must she challenge herself to do things differently?

Victoria found answers in reviewing the patterns and models in her life. They provided clues to how she knew to act as she does presently. The next steps were to learn to do things differently.

Listing all major and time-consuming tasks undertaken regularly, Victoria examined each task for the amount of energy expended on it, the importance of the task, and the tasks that could be eliminated. Further, she envisioned the way her life would change without one or more of the eliminated tasks.

VICTORIA FINALLY DID ASK FOR HER FAMILY'S HELP. THE response was acceptance and support from most of them. They did not think less of her because she needed them; it gave them a way to show their appreciation. The freeloaders disappeared.

Over the succeeding two sessions, Victoria acknowledged feelings of loneliness, hurt, anger, love, fear, and appreciation. In talking aloud about them, she confronted her vulnerability to self-disclosure. She learned to say: *I'm hurting. I need help. Help me. Hold me. Help me be safe. Thank you for helping me.* Her broken silence released the emotional weight caused by buried feelings.

AS PROPOSED INITIALLY, IN OUR EIGHTH SESSION WE REvisited our time together. There were no explicit goals but rather implicit ones dictated by the crises in Victoria's life. Medical and therapeutic interventions for her depression provided physical and emotional relief. Scripture and poetry provided spiritual nurturing. On sharing her plight, she secured support from her family. To conclude the session, Victoria responded to two questions: What have you learned? What, if anything, is unfinished for you?

"Therapy is a safe place if you have a compatible, competent therapist and the right setting," Victoria responded. "The fit has to be right or I don't think it will work as well. Initially, I was uncomfortable because I thought I had it all together and shouldn't have to see a therapist to help me. I didn't like the idea of telling a stranger about my business. I was surprised at how comfortable and peaceful it was, at times. Sometimes it was rough but I soon saw that acceptance of me as a person without judgment was a part of the process and that freed me to talk about stuff I don't talk about."

"Unfinished for you?"

"I want to understand more about myself."

"In what way?"

"It helped me to talk about things that were buried. A great weight lifted from me when I talked about them. I want to know more about me. I want to talk about my career and directions for the future."

WE AGREED TO CONTINUE AND ESTABLISHED TIMES FOR future sessions. Over the next two months, Victoria shared more

about her life situation. Her marriage had become troubled four
years before the divorce, when her spouse quit his job for no apparent reason and refused to work. Financial responsibility and
emotional support for the family had fallen onto her. She took
care of everyone's needs except her own and it wore her out.

Victoria and her husband did not talk about the situation and
she did not tell anyone about her home and work pressures. She
kept everything inside. Angry and ashamed at what was happening,
she found that her buried emotions consumed her energy. She rationalized her reactions as personal weakness and tried to maintain
her family's "public face" as a successful and problem-free family.

The home situation had not changed when Victoria tried to
talk about her distress with her husband. When he refused repeatedly to respond or expressed indifference, she shut him out of her
life physically, sexually, and emotionally. They lived in the house
for almost three years as strangers until she asked him to leave.
Victoria raised the boys alone.

Meanwhile, Victoria had struggled and coped with stress on
the job in a number of ways. To personal crises and distress, she
shut down emotionally and ran away. When hurt or distressed,
she hid her feelings behind a confident, nonchalant exterior.
Calm outside, a roaring sea inside. Victoria either responded directly to offenders or walked away from them as soon as she
could, whatever the setting. *Arrogant* and *defiant* labels followed
her, particularly at work.

However, running protected Victoria. As a child, she'd escaped
parental scolding and switching by confronting them or running

away. She shut herself away in her room. In school, she changed her schedule to escape a classmate. When a close former beau saw and approached her, she acted as if she didn't know him. She ran and internalized her distress. Unending praise for her self-control and poise rewarded and strengthened these responses.

Victoria acknowledged her discomfort at disclosing deeply personal issues before she told me about her surgery. For six months, she'd experienced irregular bleeding in her menstrual cycle with gushing-heavy flows, clots lasting up to two weeks, and alternate spotting before she reported them to her primary-care physician, who had referred her for a gynecological evaluation. The results showed tissue overgrowth on the lining of the uterus (cystic hyperplasia of the endometrium) and other abnormal uterine findings.

Seven years before, Victoria had elected a tubal ligation while having a dilation and curettage (D&C) for uterine bleeding. She had experienced pains in her lower stomach and back for many years. Victoria blamed depression for her failure to follow up with regular medical checkups after the operations, stating that she did not care whether she lived or died.

Victoria neglected her health in other ways during this problem period, gaining thirty pounds from overeating and drinking and lack of exercise. Further probes on her health status revealed links between her medical condition and depression. During the period of self-neglect, the dull, heavy aching in her lower back and abdominal pains increased. By the time she went to the doctor, her diagnosed uterine fibroids had grown to the size of grapefruits and caused her stomach to protrude.

The treatment options offered by the gynecologist included drug therapy and surgery. The drug therapy would contain the condition temporarily but also required repeated D&C procedures for an indeterminate period of time. The doctor's strongest recommendation was a complete hysterectomy in which the uterus, cervix, ovaries, and fallopian tubes would be removed. He explained that estrogen replacement therapy (ERT) would supply estrogen to her body after surgery. The pronouncement frightened Victoria because she interpreted it as drug dependency for the remainder of her life. Nevertheless, she elected to have the surgery but became increasingly dismayed as the event approached.

Victoria spent four days in the hospital and eight weeks recuperating. In research on the subject beforehand, she did not learn that alternative treatments were available to aid in her decision and did not recall the gynecologist ever mentioning alternatives, either. In talking about her surgery, intense anger surfaced.

Probes into her anger revealed castration as an issue. Through surgery she had lost her reproductive organs and a definitive part of her female identity. Some of the anger resulted from grieving the loss of her womanhood; the remainder was traced to what Victoria perceived as the physician's greed. She reasoned that the two operations involved had provided greater financial advantages for the doctor.

Urged to say more, Victoria felt the gynecologist knew the severity of her condition when he performed the first surgical procedure. Acting on the same information as before, a month later, he recommended and performed the second major surgical procedure. Victoria felt he could have considered it earlier. She was furious at his lack of sensitivity to the cumulative time she'd lost from work that resulted from his judgment.

Talking about her suppressed feelings helped Victoria come to terms with them and the resentment she transferred to the gynecologist. She owned her anger and forgave herself for the long period of inattention to her health. To dissipate more of the anger and provide closure on her surgical experiences, I encouraged her to meet with the gynecologist to discuss her remaining concerns and questions.

The proposed meeting offered an action step to drain the anger energy and redirect it in an appropriate way. Victoria did not keep her appointments the following two weeks but we maintained contact by telephone. She had refused my offer to continue the next few sessions without cost when her funds were tight. During her absence she visited the doctor and shared the information at our next meeting.

The laparoscopy and D&C performed during the first surgery, he'd told her, were diagnostic tests to examine her reproductive organs and endometrial lining for abnormalities. The results revealed a precancerous condition, the most effective treatment of which was surgical removal of the uterus, the second operation. In addition to talking with the doctor, Victoria requested her surgical reports from the hospital's medical records department. She read them, then put them in her medical file at home.

Victoria commented, "The most amazing thing is how I never heard anyone say anything about their hysterectomies. After I had mine, almost every other woman I talked to had undergone the surgery. I was shocked. I feel a little better now that I have talked with the doctor. I still have an attitude about the castration issue and how it is ignored. I feel strongly that Black women should talk more openly about it."

I suggested that she might want to consider ways to address the issue and her role in making it happen.

We redirected our focus to alternative ways to cope with distress personally and in interactions with others by considering the factors she can and cannot control. She could control her attitudes, behavior, and responses, and in doing so change others' responses to her. She cannot always change her environment but can change her responses to it. She can know that options always exist and can choose from them.

Victoria applied the concept to her career. Her status as a certified public accountant (CPA) placed her in a favorable position to generate career options. Three included teaming with other CPAs to form a joint practice; joining an established firm; and establishing a home-based, professional practice. Victoria realized that while none would likely make her a millionaire, certainly she could feel safe in her career.

At the termination of Victoria's individual therapy, I recommended an African American support group for her to continue her personal growth and to strengthen new behavior. The lawsuit against the agency was pending. The agency had approached her attorney to negotiate a settlement, but no decision had been reached. Victoria collected unemployment insurance to stabilize her finances until she joined a CPA firm. Eventually, she planned to establish a home-based practice as a CPA.

★   ★   ★

VICTORIA'S EXPERIENCE IS NOT AN ISOLATED INCIDENT. I'VE heard the same story hundreds of times. Black women at all levels face job ceilings. I faced them in my own work experience. Do these environmental circumstances create a perpetual state of frustration in Black women? The answers are yes and no. Yes, if we try to penetrate these ceilings with our fingertips and accept them as limits to our potential to work creatively and productively. No, if we recognize that there are other ways to create satisfying and productive outlets for our abilities, training, and experience.

Individually and in teams, more Black women are moving their careers along as entrepreneurs with home-based and other businesses, professional practices, and the like. They are creating safe and satisfying careers for themselves. This is where personal balance comes into play. The development of the spiritual, mental, and physical aspects of ourselves helps to avoid perpetual states of frustration and to grow positively. Cultivating one or two of these aspects will not do. It takes all three to restore balance.

FOUR

Steel Ceilings, Not Glass

LIMITED ADVANCEMENT FOR BLACK WOMEN HAS ALWAYS existed. Many intelligent, articulate, educated women of color find themselves trapped in low-paying, low-status jobs. Not only is access often denied, but frequently we have no clue about the career possibilities and lifestyles at higher levels. These career ceilings are not made of glass, they are made of steel. With glass ceilings, the places to move up can at least be seen. Frustration comes from the inability to penetrate them. Even then, the possibility of breaking the glass still exists. Some Black women are under glass ceilings, but most are not.

With steel ceilings, there is neither the view nor the access upward beyond a certain point. It is like climbing the stairs of a twenty-story building and finding no door to enter the top floor. Steel ceilings are those impenetrable barriers to positions, privileges, and accompanying lifestyles at higher levels. Productive on the job, diligent in service, and called upon to be better qualified and work harder than White counterparts, most Black women find it impossible to advance beyond certain levels.

Racial and sexual harassment is still reported regularly, even with laws in place to prevent it. Black women also find themselves singled out and treated differently. It is commonplace to enter work sites and face climates that broadcast misgivings about our selection and ability to do the job, especially within management positions. For some Black women, isolation and the withholding of resources, personnel assistance, and vital information create no-win situations, which support prejudgments that we are incompetent. Other women complain that our management authority is an illusion, with decisions commonly undermined or overridden.

It is not uncommon for Black women to find work environments unsupportive. Many are more like proving grounds for the expectations of others who believe that our unworthiness to do the job will eventually show. While it is reasonable for employers to expect competence, it is equally reasonable to expect the support and resources normally provided to employees for successful job performance.

The abusive tactics used to intimidate, exclude, and fire Black women penalize and hurt many who perform consistently at and above standards. Reasons for termination range from insubordination and attitude to ethnic hairstyle and dress distractions. Sometimes no reason or explanation is given at all.

Growing numbers of Black women employed in middle and upper management and others in lower-level positions are enter-

ing therapy to vent their frustrations, fortify their coping strategies, and develop stress management plans. Nora was one of them.

THE CEO OF A SMALL PRIVATE-MANAGEMENT COMPANY
recruited thirty-eight-year-old Nora to fill a vice president's position on his staff. She became the only woman and only person
of color on a senior staff composed of fourteen White males. The
two other African Americans in the 350-employee company were
female secretaries. One was a twenty-three-year-old high school
graduate; the other, a thirty-five-year-old former teacher who
hoped her business management master's degree would help move
her into a management position.

The CEO and Nora met during their appointments as Planning Commission board members and worked together on several citywide projects. Impressed with her skills and personality,
he persuaded Nora to direct similar projects at his company. Tap-
ping her for the job was not a difficult choice. She stood out.

Extremely attractive, poised, and stunning in her designer suits
and shoes, Nora moved comfortably among her peers. Her skirts,
worn just above the knee, exposed firm, shapely legs from years
of running. Nora's quiet manner often misled those who tried to
overpower her. Behind the reserve were formidable strength and
a quick wit, both of which enabled her to handle confrontational
situations.

She and her older sister—their parents' pride and joy—were
reared in a tightly knit extended family and given every advantage

the family could provide. Both followed the family's tradition of education, achievement, and deportment. Grandparents on both sides earned master's degrees and worked with distinction in their respective fields and the community. Nora's parents and sister earned terminal professional degrees in health fields and also performed volunteer service.

Nora traveled a long road to reach her vice president's position. She taught high school for three years before entering graduate school full-time to earn the master of business administration (MBA) degree. For thirteen years, she held a variety of positions in city and federal government while active in community affairs.

In more than one of the positions, Nora faced steel ceilings in her efforts to advance. Jolted to find she was the first African American hired to a ten-member specialty federal service branch after five years in city government, Nora hoped her challenges would be minor. The prospect faded when she saw that the bond and information exchange among the seven White male staff members excluded the two females, each of whom worked independently. Nora quickly experienced isolation within the staff but continued to study the agency's culture to see how to best perform her job and to advance. Nora was prepared. (Only she, the director, and another coworker—both males—held MBA degrees.)

The work was mostly uncomplicated. Clearly defined agency guidelines and a performance agreement helped her to adjust. As initial staff reservations and sporadic hostility toward her eased, Nora redirected to her work the energy previously used to counteract those forces.

Without exception, she earned superior ratings, conducted agencywide staff development training, and presented workshops at national conventions. Yet officials repeatedly passed over her applications for the upper-level management training program and chose not to acknowledge them. Two years of neglect were enough for Nora to seek advancement opportunities elsewhere.

She received an offer to fill a newly created position as special assistant to an agency administrator. This position meant a salary increase from her current job. Ironically, the director of her current job made several attempts to prevent Nora from leaving. He called the receiving agency to declare her ineligibility for the position as special assistant on grounds that she had not spent the required time in her present grade level. Nora's higher civil service rating in her field refuted the claim. He searched her employment record and lifted conflicting employment dates to charge record falsification as a reason to revoke her federal employment. Nora negated the charge with documents that proved legitimate, concurrent employment. His dirty tricks continued until she left.

Nora fit well in the new work setting. She and the administrator complemented and respected each other. However, three years of smooth sailing shifted when a White female contract employee selected to work on a special project troubled the waters. From the outset, the woman paid more attention to Nora's duties and to achieving permanent status than to the project for which she was hired. Her efforts to undermine Nora's authority and gain the administrator's ear succeeded. Exclusion from meetings and information flow, incomplete data for reports, and open hostility followed. The obstacles frustrated Nora and required extra energy to stay focused and perform her job at her previous superior levels.

Ten months passed before the administrator and personnel discovered that the woman's propensity to lie crossed work, personal, and social boundaries. Work on the project suffered, and they terminated her. Nora spent two months cleaning up the mess and fulfilled the responsibilities and duties of both positions for another year. The administrator rewarded her efforts with a five-thousand-dollar bonus, but the tide shifted again when he transferred to another agency at the year's end.

Shortly after the new administrator's arrival, he announced the reorganization of the department into two sections. Since Nora functioned in two positions, she expected to be appointed the leader. It didn't happen. A few times, Nora came to work early and saw she had been excluded from the administrator's meetings. After several weeks of shunning, a new man appeared on the scene without notice or introduction. He bore the same title as Nora, but she continued to perform the work of two people. The meetings included him but still excluded her.

When the administrator finally ordered Nora to report to the new man (hired at a higher salary), continue to perform the duties of two people, and teach him her job, she knew it was time for her to go. The pressure and demands intensified before she found another position a year later. They included isolation, requests for last-minute busywork reports and weekend work, withholding information needed to complete assignments accurately, and contemptuous tones of voice when addressing her.

Nora faced staying in the bad situation or leaving. She prepared to move on but it seemed that the cycle would never end. Even though she continued to get promising positions, they all had impenetrable steel ceilings.

After several satisfying relationships, Nora considered marriage but put it on the back burner to pursue her career. When she stopped to assess her time and progress, she had turned forty. Her life was devoted to work and volunteer activity. Work consumed most of it, especially this current position at the management company.

"The pressure is getting to me," exclaimed Nora, accentuating every other word. "Ninety thousand a year plus expenses is the most money I have ever made, but I am more miserable than I have ever been in my whole life. Every day is filled with tension, trying to get my work done, dealing with personalities and egos, and one-upmanship. I have something to do every minute of the day and that day is long. I'm not talking nine-to-five. I'm talking nine-to-nine, nine-to-eight. Then I'm subject to being called back to work when I'm off."

Nora quickly inhaled and exhaled. Emphasizing each word, she continued. "I can do my job. That's not a problem. It's the other stuff that's getting next to me. My social life is shot and I'm not getting any younger. The job was okay the first two years because it was different and I traveled. I went to places I never thought I would go—in the United States and abroad—and with expense accounts. I met a lot of interesting people, too, but the novelty soon wore off."

Additional stress came from the constant microscopic scrutiny;

the biases; the innuendoes about her ability and the quality of her work; and the questions about how she'd gotten the position. Nora was excluded from the White male camaraderie and support that bolstered their confidence. Despite her abilities, education, and experience, Nora's coworkers searched for areas to criticize, often brutally.

"I'm not sure why I expected the behavior to be better in the private sector but it's the same old thing. They look for weak spots to push my buttons and try to make me break. I was sensitive in the beginning because of the isolation. It's harder to be at your best when someone constantly throws darts at you. After a while, it messes a little with your confidence. I guess that's what it's supposed to do. I found myself holding back when I knew I had relevant contributions. I was reluctant to offer them. It was that confidence thing. I started second-guessing myself—that was before I figured out what was going on.

"It's painful, though. You try to do right, be upstanding and that sort of thing, but penalties keep coming. You think that after you toil for so long, there might be some relief from the flagrant racism and sexism—but I guess not."

Therapy offered a neutral place for Nora to talk about what was happening to her and to review her coping skills. She needed to confirm her perceptions, her conclusions, and the impact of the workplace. We discussed these concerns and revisited her career goals in sixteen sessions that extended over six months because of out-of-town work obligations.

Normally, Nora vented concerns with her mother and sister

in regular telephone calls home. The contacts comforted her, particularly during stressful times, since she lived alone in a different state. Her father had provided strong support before he died a few years earlier. Grandparents on both sides were ever ready to listen, share their experience, and offer advice and encouragement.

Nora had seen her move to the company as an opportunity to expand contacts in the private sector. Though initially excited about her vice president status, she soon learned that it carried no real authority. From day one, Nora walked into a maze of power plays.

One or another effort to control Nora, make her appear incompetent, or both filled each day. During the transition from the old job to the current one, important interoffice memoranda needed to prepare Nora for staff meetings frequently disappeared from her mail. The draft of an article—prepared at the CEO's request for publication in the company paper—was taken from her office, defaced with large red marks, and circulated throughout the senior staff. During a staff meeting, a colleague asked Nora to prepare graphs, although the company employed a full-time graphic arts person.

Moreover, Nora did not have access to the many informal lunch and dinner discussions outside the office. Ideas she proposed in planning meetings often resurfaced later in different formats, without acknowledgment that they had originated with her. Colleagues gave Nora's staff assistants counterassignments and reassignments without her knowledge. Questions about the actions summoned feigned ignorance or denials.

More than once, Nora walked into impromptu meetings from which she was excluded. One was about bonuses, as she later discovered when the CEO slipped her an envelope containing six hundred dollars in cash. Bonuses had been awarded earlier to the other senior staff members. Nora never knew how much.

Another male colleague refused to acknowledge Nora's presence with greetings, never addressed her directly in or out of staff meetings, and repeatedly spewed caustic remarks about the projects she directed. Yet at more than one office social, she had to rebuff his inappropriate advances and those of another coworker who drank too much alcohol at the functions.

The women in Nora's family warned her about the sexual harassment and innuendoes she would face as an attractive African American woman. They also schooled her on how to handle and respond to them. There were unending barriers and offenses, blatant criticism, and ridicule. Nora faced some form of them throughout her four-year stay at the company.

Several factors helped Nora to cope in the environment. Foremost, family nurturing and training instilled a strong sense of self and confidence in her abilities. Family and friends offered emotional support and outlets to vent and relax. The quality of interactions and experiences at the historically black university Nora attended nourished her self-esteem and also prepared her to face obstacles in the larger work and social worlds. And finally, experience in the work world itself helped Nora to survive.

Beyond confirming the accuracy of her perceptions and conclusions, we directed our attention to quality-of-life issues and their implications for the remainder of her career. Nora began by answering self-examination questions. She would revisit them throughout the course of therapy and beyond, as needed.

- What do I want for myself and my career?
- What are the considerations?
- What am I overlooking?
- What am I neglecting?
- What is fun for me?
- Is fun included in my lifestyle?
- What drives me and why?
- How am I taking care of myself?
- What stressors do I need to watch during this week?
- How am I caring for my physical self? What do I need to do? When do I plan to do it?
- How am I caring for my spiritual self? What do I need to do? When do I plan to do it?
- How am I caring for my emotional self? What do I need to do? When do I plan to do it?
- What is my legacy?
- What do I want to change?

Nora identified control of her time, freedom to be creative, and a small work setting as the most important elements for a satisfying job. She redefined her career goals to pursue them in a self-owned management firm where she could use her skills, experience, and contacts. Nora set a two-year limit to stay with the company and concentrated on how to best use the remaining time. The decision, a means to an end, helped her to stay focused and to tolerate her colleagues.

She concentrated on policies and procedures, technical and business plans, forms of incorporation, and applicable taxes. Nora looked at staffing and staff organization, marketing and incentives, equipment and supplies, office space, and budgets. Evaluation and sound financial planning prepared Nora to leave her job. Each week in therapy, she identified her learning and areas for improvement and kept track of them in her journal.

When I asked her about significant insights from her experience with the company, Nora replied that she'd seen in action the saying, "Two heads are better than one." She valued seeing how the senior staff pooled their talent and experience to produce the best possible product. She planned to use the technique to manage and build teams in her own company.

Nora also understood her family's warning that some things come with the territory. Reactions to her African American female status are facts of life. She knows also that her personal worth exceeds the dynamics and negative behavior displayed toward her at work or in any setting. Nora brought her personal attributes and experience to the company; they were not developed there. She retained her strength through physical, mental, and spiritual nurturing, traits modeled in her family. Attending to each aspect provided the balance that maintained her during difficult periods.

Nora's outlook for the future was promising. Family and friends provided emotional support. She accessed financial support through institutional, family, and her own resources. Nora possessed the planning and organizational skills, determination, and drive to implement a successful venture. Certainty on what she needed allowed her to stay on the job until she was ready to implement her plans. She made the best of her situation and used her time productively.

NORA MAINTAINED CONTACT WITH ME THROUGH OCCA-sional telephone calls. She left the company after two years. I received an invitation to a chamber of commerce dinner honoring her as entrepreneur of the year. She included a newspaper clipping featuring a picture of her mother, sister, and her in a successful joint venture.

FIVE

Cleaning Up My Act

"IT SEEMS THAT ALL THE GOOD MEN ARE ALREADY MAR-ried. I mean Black men. The others are gay, in prison, or don't want to commit to a relationship," complained Kate during her initial interview. The gifted twenty-nine-year-old singer was tired of running and wanted to create stability in her life and relationships with men. She punished herself because of failed relationships and had entered therapy to find out why they never lasted.

On meeting a guy, Kate plunged into a whirlwind dating spree with him. If the vibes were right, their first date ended with sex at his place or hers. She was influenced by money, good looks-dress-car, smooth talk, height over the five feet six inches that she stood, and a wine-and-dine routine. When Kate targeted a man as a prospective mate, she became a receptacle for his wishes with no boundaries for their association. She provided sex on demand; bought him gifts; accepted his calls and visits at any hour; and telephoned him regularly at work and home whether he returned the calls or not.

After a few weeks, Kate was inevitably no longer interesting and her rating with the man fell to D. Dates and invitations to social functions stopped. The romance fizzled. After that, their contacts were primarily sexual and time with Kate was spent at her apartment.

Kate rationalized her accommodating behavior as "being there" for the man, thinking it would motivate him to appreciate her. The message she sent, however, was *treat-me-as-you-please-because-I-have-no-boundaries.* Occasionally, he turned to her and stayed the night when down and needing a sympathetic ear. This pattern recurred often until the man left her life completely.

Kate's last partner had hurt her deeply. She'd moved in with him shortly after they met and stayed with him for six months. She interpreted their length of time together as a commitment that would eventually lead to marriage. He assessed the situation differently. He wanted to end their association but did not discuss it with Kate. Instead, he showed it in his attitude and behavior. Constant fault-finding remarks about her looks, size, and manners demeaned and undermined her confidence. Exclusion from several important events in his life hurt and embarrassed her.

The good times and fun changed after a few months. He stood Kate up when they planned to go out and thought nothing of staying away through the night without a word to her. When she saw him again, he flaunted indifference or barked that he had something else to do. Kate hurt when he talked on the telephone in her presence or left to talk in another room. The rebuffs continued when he refused to return her calls from work, especially when absent all night.

Alternately, Kate tolerated his treatment, explained away his behavior, and confronted him until too humiliated to continue. When he'd asked Kate to leave during their last bout, she'd felt terrible and believed something was wrong with her.

Kate's girlfriends added to her distress by criticizing and disclosing the antics of her boyfriends over the years. They had watched Kate grow as a featured singer with the high school jazz band and choir and feared that romantic involvement would detract from achieving her career goals as a singer.

Finances had prevented Kate from attending college, even though she wasn't sure how college would help her. No one in her family went to college. At any rate, the lack of scholarship offers or advice about financial resources had closed the matter. After graduation, Kate held conventional day jobs and sang at night. Most recently, she had worked as a receptionist and intermittently appeared nights and weekends at local clubs. She met and attracted many men.

Near the session's end, I encouraged Kate to examine the dynamics in her relationships with men. I asked her to identify three prior relationships she valued and answer the following questions:

- What attracted the men to her?

- What did they bring to the relationship?

- What did she expect from them?

- In what ways were her expectations communicated to them?

- What did she bring to the relationships?

As we reviewed our time together, Kate noted how quickly the time passed and how much more she had to tell me. I urged her to use the journal to record her thoughts for our next meeting. I announced that our time was up, stood until Kate joined me, and walked her to the door.

THE NEXT TIME I SAW KATE, A BLACK LYCRA BODYSUIT AND oversized black suede vest covered Kate's shapely size-eight figure. Her cropped, naturally curly black hair exposed a one-carat-diamond stud in each ear. Black leather shoe boots and a shoulder bag completed her outfit. Kate strutted in, sat, and crossed her legs.

"Go, girl," I commented on her appearance.

"It's my go-to-hell outfit. Makes me feel powerful."

I looked quizzically.

"When I feel vulnerable, it gives me a boost—a boost I need."

"Vulnerable?"

"My man situation. You know. The reactions I get let me know I still have it. Yeah, but I know it's not enough. It doesn't last."

"It's okay. That's one of the reasons why you're here—to find out why. Where do you want to begin?"

Kate talked about her singing engagements and how well she

had been received. As she described the events, Kate remarked casually that a former mate had been at one of the receptions with another woman. Without pause, she rambled on about the events in detail.

At one point, I leaned toward Kate. "You tried to slip that one past me. What happened?"

"He walked around the room with her on his arm, greeting people he knew. He didn't even speak to me. In fact, he acted like he didn't know me."

"What did you do?"

"Nothing. I was in too much pain."

"Pain?"

"Yes. Humiliated, hurt, rejected. You name it. I can't see how he can just walk away from me like there was never anything between us. I know he enjoyed being with me. I did all I could to please him."

"What did you overlook?"

Kate laid her head back and gazed at the ceiling for a while before she spoke. "I was so busy trying to make our relationship work that I forgot about me. I guess I acted desperate." Kate's crossed legs swung rapidly in and out.

"I thought that by this age, I would be successful in my career, married, and maybe raising a family. I never imagined that it wouldn't be that way. Now I find myself eyeing my biological clock and on the verge of panic about everything. It pisses me off . . . and it makes me sad. What did I overlook? Myself." She whispered. "I overlooked myself."

"It hurts."

"Something awful. I've got to do better than this. The parade's not going down this street anymore. What do I do next?"

"Come to terms with the pain. It might not seem like it now but the pain will eventually go away."

"Yeah. Right."

"It will. Pain is a normal, human emotion. It lets us know that we are alive and warns us that something is not right. The way we cope with pain depends on our attitudes toward it. Look at it as an opportunity to learn more about yourself—and to treat yourself better."

With her arms folded, Kate sat motionless for two minutes (a long time in therapy) before saying, "Next."

Inquiry into her attractions and expectations of male companions revealed Kate's preference for dashing, street-smart dudes with cash. Their surface qualities and lifestyle strongly attracted her, and she acted solely on feelings when they got together. Kate ignored other considerations that laid the foundation for a lasting relationship. When a man met her criteria and treated her well, she interpreted it as his readiness to commit to a long-term relationship and assumed that as time passed, their feelings toward each other would deepen. It was clear that her expectations differed from theirs.

Kate's expectations were visions of what she saw happening in her interactions with men (and other people) and their interactions with her. Her expectations, like ours, incorporated the attitudes, beliefs, and behaviors that she considered to be right. She internalized them from her experiences, family, and society, and they influenced how she interpreted issues and life events.

When both parties in a relationship know what is expected of each other, the values important to both are clear. Clarity eliminates assumptions about what one person ought to know about the other person's needs and wants. The understanding creates the open, honest communication needed for a sound relationship.

Kate hadn't thought much about expectations or what went into building a relationship. Meeting the right man and getting married was something that just happened.

"I didn't think I had to plan for anything. I see other women with men and good relationships and I say what's wrong with me? Why can't I have someone to love me? Someone who is devoted to me? I'm a good person."

"What messages do you give to the men you choose?"

"What do you mean?"

"How you act with them. Your behavior tells a lot about how you feel about yourself and what you expect from the man."

"I don't know. I guess I've been too anxious."

"Anything else?"

"I assumed too much about how he really felt about me. I acted on my feelings about him and what I wanted him to feel about me. I misread him."

"Misread?"

"I let him use me."

"So you haven't placed value on yourself. You've let the men in your life do it."

"Yes, but there is so much competition. If I don't another woman will."

"So what. Take yourself out of the competition. It wouldn't be any worse than it is now." I paused for emphasis then asked, "What do you hear me saying to you?"

"I have to be responsible for my happiness. Things won't get any better for me until I value myself. That will keep me from being desperate." Kate lapsed into thought. "That's easier for you to say, you already have a career. You're already married and have been. You didn't have to deal with competition."

"Listen. The dynamics between men and women are not new with you or me. That kind of competition began in the garden of Eden with Adam, Eve, and Satan. It is about our core values and what we do with them that make the difference. That's what we are working on."

DURING THE NEXT TWO SESSIONS, WE CONTINUED TO EX- amine Kate's expectations of men in relationships. Drama and rescue recurred as issues. Her preference for dashing men with excitement represented a fireworks expectation. I called it a "Fourth of July" expectation because the value placed on the re- lationship was gauged by the amount of drama created and expe- rienced in it.

The drama in those relationships unfolded from competition with another woman, other women, or friends involved with the men. It was also created in the demands made on Kate's time and accountability or in extravagant or otherwise extraordinary life- styles. Sometimes power and control issues that took the form of threats or actual physical violence created the drama.

All forms of the drama rang true for Kate. She had wondered why it was difficult to appreciate and maintain relationships with "nice" men. (The quiet, ordinary, maybe-religious, sometimes-homely-sometimes-handsome, educated-or-uneducated, steady-job-holding men.) She perceived them as good potential husbands who treated her decently, but she couldn't get into them.

For Kate, and other women like her, these men did not create enough excitement. They didn't supply the drama. I suggested that it might be beneficial to revisit what she'd overlooked in them. Fireworks create a beautiful, noisy display but don't last long and leave a mess after they burn out.

Kate's preference for dashing, exciting men also suggested an expectation to be rescued. "Mr. Right"—this ideal man with money, good looks, good job, and know-how—would come and carry her away as if she were Cinderella. Not always on a conscious level, the fantasy may just be an escape for many Black women from the past and present negative messages received about themselves from society.

Kate recognized the quality-of-life issues and the need to examine them. I also posed ongoing, related questions and asked Kate to answer them once in her journal and again periodically in therapy:

- Do I want a life that is inferior to what I deserve and can create?
- Am I asking too much?
- What are my bottom lines?

- Do I feel that I am nothing without a man who expects me to surrender my identity to him?

- In what ways can I create a fulfilling life?

- Do I believe that I can do it?

- What do I want?

Questions about how she was raised to act toward men also helped Kate to understand her present behavior and empowered her to make desired changes.

Kate's father, it turned out, had never married her mother. Shortly after her birth, he married another woman and fathered three more children. Kate's mother worked to support the family. She did not consider court-ordered child support an option and took whatever he doled out without complaint. Even before Kate was born, she gave to him endlessly, thinking it would inspire his love and commitment. It did not. Instead, her habitual giving allowed him to take more emotionally and financially than he gave.

Kate's contacts with her father were limited to his random visits, when he assumed the center stage and engaged everyone around him. Her mother sprang to action, anticipating and anxious to fulfill his every request. Kate watched her mother respond to this tall, handsome, well-dressed, sweet-talking charmer who brought cheer, laughter, and excitement with his visits.

For homework, I asked Kate to study how her mother related to her father and other males; to describe the interactions; and to identify similar patterns in her life.

* * *

SADNESS AND DISAPPOINTMENT ENVELOPED KATE AT OUR next weekly session. Pain rose to the surface of her face when she talked about again running into her former companion between visits. However, acknowledging rather than hiding the pain made it a little less intense. Kate didn't dwell on him or the pain. After talking about both enough to lift her mood, she moved to her journal entries.

"My assignment was uncomfortable. I had to confront my family situation. Facing it was painful." Kate's shoulders dropped. *"Whew."* She gently blew while shaking her head. "Shame. I was always ashamed. Everybody in town knew about my mom and dad but nobody talked about it. My mom didn't either. Nobody mistreated me, everybody just knew. Me and one of his daughters could go for twins. We're a year apart."

Kate paused a few seconds. "But you know, talking about my father is a relief because I've been carrying stuff about him around for a long time. I took a good look at my parents and I'm really kinda doing what my mom did—just with more than one man. Searchin' for love, I suppose. She didn't have boundaries either—let my father walk over her. She let him get away with murder."

"What's unfinished for you?"

"Whys. Why did this happen? Why did that happen?"

"What meaning is there for you?"

"Finding my own whys. I've got to continue to find the answers to my whys. I can't do anything about hers."

"Sounds all right to me. Where do habit and routine fit into your pattern of relating to men?"

"I don't know. I'm not clear about the difference."

"Look them up." I passed a dictionary to Kate.

She leafed through and found both terms. "*Habit* is a subconscious act that is repeated. *Routine* is a conscious act that is planned and carried out." Kate looked up. "What do they have to do with me?"

"What do they have to do with you? Look at your associations and see how they apply to you."

After a pause Kate answered. "I guess I give out of habit, hoping that I'll get the same thing back." She spoke absently, as if to herself. "Why do I keep giving? Because that's what I know." Pause. "Routine? That must be the point. I plan and carry out what I know. Okay."

"True. To change, you have to learn to do something different."

Kate overextended herself to men and settled for what they gave. This pattern of male-and-female interactions, modeled in her family, bred low self-esteem and feelings that she had no alternatives. The strong need for acceptance underlay her self-defeating behavior even when males' lack of appreciation hurt and humiliated her. Kate wanted her love returned but didn't know how to get it.

IN THE FOLLOWING SESSION, AS WE DELVED FURTHER INTO the nature of her contacts with men, Kate bristled when I suggested they were not truly relationships. The whirlwind dating filled with things to do and the immediate sexual contact without attention to relationship building represented forced friendships. They had no substance. I saw them as someone's definition of fun. Maybe the man's, maybe Kate's, maybe both.

Protesting loudly, Kate pronounced me old-fashioned and out of touch. Continuing without pause, she announced that everyone did it. Further assertions about liberated women and relationships in the new millennium spewed along with pitches about her biological needs that had to be met. I acknowledged okay when she asked if I understood.

We watched each other for a few moments until I asked what was involved in building a relationship. What happened when she became sexually intimate with a man before she knew anything about him? Kate ignored my questions and continued to defend her position for the remainder of our session. I listened without comment. At the end, I recommended that she continue the behavior if it worked for her. If not, consider my questions.

The probes and resistance continued at our next meeting. I intervened with a doormat/crystal analogy. The doormat reflected negative treatment; crystal reflected self-worth and appreciation.

"What is the purpose of a doormat?" I asked Kate.

She answered immediately. "To catch the dirt tracked in from outside."

"What is the life of a doormat?"

"Uh, it's taken for granted. You don't notice it—it doesn't attract attention. Oh. It never talks back. It doesn't take care of itself."

"The doormat stays where it's put to serve others."

Kate gazed intently at me as I continued to question her.

"What else?"

Tears formed and overflowed on Kate's cheeks. "It doesn't show dirt—or abuse."

"The doormat gets attention only when it is too worn and no longer useful. Then it's thrown away."

Kate commented somberly. "All a doormat is good for is walking on."

"Yes. Acceptance of poor treatment reflects how we feel about ourselves. It tells other persons with whom we are in contact that their behavior is acceptable and can be continued. Continuous negative messages lower our self-esteem."

We sat silently as Kate reached for tissue to pat her eyes.

She spoke. "I recognize myself and it doesn't feel good."

I sat quietly as Kate continued to cry.

Blotting her eyes, she asked, "What about the crystal? You can go on. I'm okay."

"Well, most of the same questions apply. How do you treat fine crystal?"

"Take care of it because you appreciate it."

"How do you treat fine crystal when you use it?"

"Handle it with care; hand-wash it, and put it back in the china cabinet."

"Crystal is returned to a place of honor where it can be seen and admired. It's valued and treated special. Fine crystal won't tolerate neglect and mistreatment."

Kate dabbed at the unbroken flow of tears. She felt exposed but aware that her relationships with men could not continue as they had. I offered questions for her reflection and journal writing.

- At what times do you allow yourself to be treated like a doormat?
- At what times do you allow yourself to be treated like fine crystal?
- What constructive changes can you make in your attitude and behavior?
- What implicit and explicit messages do you send to a man about yourself when you engage in casual sex?
- How accurate are the messages?
- Are they the messages you intend to send?
- In what ways can you reflect changes in how you treat yourself?
- In what ways can you reflect changes in how you treat your mate?

My concluding statement to Kate was a bottom line. When we value ourselves, other people will value us. The opposite is also true. If we do not place a high value on ourselves, others will not place a high value on us either.

★   ★   ★

IN SUBSEQUENT SESSIONS, WE EXTENDED THE EVALUATION of Kate's behavior and its consequences. She repeated her behavior in interactions with other people and confirmed that they often took advantage of her. There were no boundaries for them either. We weighed how the people in our lives choose how they will act toward us when we do not establish boundaries for their behavior. They define how they will treat us. When this happens, our control is outside of us and with them.

To reclaim personal control, Kate worked to improve her choices. She began the process by analyzing several difficult situations previously faced. For each situation, she evaluated her responses to see if they had achieved the results she wanted.

Kate also identified several other ways to respond to the same situation and weighed each for appropriateness in achieving better results. She chose best when she stopped to consider the several possibilities and selected from them. Kate recognized that more than one solution existed for any problem. I encouraged her to apply the principle to future situations.

The process helped Kate to understand that there are always alternatives and she can always choose to act differently. I reminded her that she could not change other people but she could change their responses to her.

With exceptions during holidays and for other valid reasons, Kate attended sessions for eight months. Between them, she applied her learning to situations she encountered. Initial awkwardness eased as she gained experience. Kate discovered the key: Changes in her behavior prompted different behavior toward her from others.

Pleased and excited at a later session, Kate described some of the changes in her behavior during the past months. When a former acquaintance she didn't like much called and asked to come over, Kate's old behavior kicked in and she agreed to meet him at seven-thirty that evening. Kate knew he wanted sex. Those were the only times he called. Ordinarily, she would have gone ahead, knowing she wouldn't see him until he wanted sex again, but when he came by at ten-thirty that night she couldn't do it. The messages spun in her head: *You don't want this. You don't have to settle for this.*

After he arrived, they greeted and hugged before Kate went to make drinks for them. This time, she brought coffee from the kitchen instead of the usual cocktails. His surprised look betrayed his calm as he asked what was going on with her. She knew what he meant because, before, they would have been in bed by then. Kate sat and told him about her singing career and new work projects. She asked about his job and mutual friends. They chatted and laughed for about forty minutes more before he moved closer to rub his hand down her thigh. She stood abruptly and went for more coffee.

Standing when she returned, he took the coffee and responded to her small talk for twenty more minutes before bowing out. Kate had asked him to call again when he wanted to go out but hadn't heard from him since.

From the experience, Kate realized she didn't have to be desperate. There could be a relationship without trying to win a man over with sex. It stung, though, to know she had allowed herself to be at that place.

In responding to the earlier question on relationship building, she concluded that it involved getting to know someone, so that being together was not just about sex. Also, a relationship required honesty and clarity about each party's expectations. The revelations empowered her and, for the moment, she felt better.

Kate imposed a moratorium on her old behavior with males. With support in therapy, she incorporated elements of relationship building as requirements to maintain her self-respect. The qualities laid the foundation for friendship whether it led to a long-term romantic relationship or not. It was a decision she always had to make about her behavior with men.

In later sessions, Kate talked about the void and loneliness that accompanied the changes in her behavior where emptiness, sadness, and hurt had once been. They were grief responses to the loss of her last relationship. She was vulnerable. Memories of life with her partner did not automatically disappear when the relationship ended. Kate's attempts to erase them immediately and be over it intensified her grief.

Kate needed to understand that grieving time varies from person to person. Her emotions, though intense and raw, would eventually heal unless she picked at them continuously—that is, wallowed in sorrow or tried to relight a connection that no longer existed. Kate faced acknowledging the pain and moving on with her life or increasing the pain by trying to deny it. I emphasized *trying* because pain will not be denied. It resurfaces in other, usually destructive forms.

For solutions to her dilemma, Kate looked at how she spent weekdays and weekends. Duties and contact with people at work filled weekdays, but she was alone without plans on the nights and weekends when she did not sing.

Next, Kate identified all the things she most enjoyed doing. After placing them into categories of people to see, places to go, and things to do, she matched them with opportunities that were available. Many suitable possibilities resulted, like museum visits, because she enjoyed them immensely, as well as shows at theaters and local universities. To the assignment, Kate added neglected friends and the standard invitations to events she ignored routinely. Learning to play the guitar emerged as the favorite thing to do at home alone.

For the next step, Kate planned in detail how to spend weekends and holidays and recorded them on a large wall calendar. It provided constant visual reminders until she adopted the new lifestyle. Even though the plans sometimes changed, it was important not to leave them to chance, especially with loneliness as a problem. Planning leisure time worked.

I suggested that attention to others during loneliness helps to ease it. A call, visit, or errand for an elderly person living alone or visit to a teen group home or some other goodwill action can shift the focus from herself to another. The point was to do something for someone else.

For volunteer activity, Kate identified organizations that offered career opportunities and called for information and written material. Preparation for participation began with understanding that people are at different places in their reception and responses to new members. Clarity on why she chose to volunteer at the organization and what she took to it was essential. How to observe intergroup dynamics and identify questions to ask also prepared her. After initial anxiety, Kate grew more confident as she approached and engaged in new activity.

In our remaining sessions, Kate reviewed her time in therapy for significant learning and application to life situations. First and foremost, she recognized her worth as a person to be loved and respected. When she treated herself well, the people with whom she associated followed suit. Taking care of herself physically and emotionally showed self-respect and provided a model for those who wanted to be in a relationship with her. It also helped to revise Kate's mental tapes that said being unmarried meant unhappiness. For personal goals, she chose to concentrate on her singing career, develop her spiritual life, and continue to define wholesome fun.

Kate maintained a journal and completed selected readings as homework assignments throughout therapy. Reading and writing about her issues, emotions, reactions, and insights kept her actively engaged in the therapeutic process beyond our sessions. I encouraged her to continue them after our sessions ended.

Probing the issues and their sources began our journey. Understanding her motives and roles in relationships empowered Kate to redefine how to function in future relationships. She built a strong support network in which she tried new behavior and received feedback on it. Kate planned her moves and took one step at a time.

The examination of dynamics between two parties was my answer to Kate's question on how to tell if the potential for a relationship existed. Pay close attention to the actions each takes toward the other for clues. Words alone do not tell the whole story.

Emotions (or feelings) in a relationship are not static. On a horizontal continuum they range from one extreme of love to the other extreme of hate. Both extremes and the variations between them contain elements of concern. Sometimes the gap between love and hate is not that big. We often love those we hate, and hate the ones we love. When we involve our emotions, whether positively or negatively, it shows how much we care about the relationship. When there is no longer caring in a relationship, the emotion is indifference.

Continuous negative acts blunt the emotions and make us feel indifferent. There is no longer a relationship when consistent inconsideration and indifference dominate. There is meaningless game playing and pain.

When the issues in a relationship are clear, communicated, and understood, the courses of action are clear. We can choose options that will help us to work through difficulties in relationships or end them and move on to more satisfying relationships.

Still, some of us never want to be clear about our issues. We'll either die with them or take our baggage to someone else and repeat the negative, destructive patterns. Invariably, dysfunction results, appearing as low self-esteem, depression, anxiety, guilt, fear, mood swings, and unhealthy emotional responses in relationships.

Issues of power and control surface in all types of relationships.

It is within us to act effectively and treat others as we want to be treated. When we do, we are in control of ourselves, and that is enough. It provides a model for partners, if they choose to use it. If not, they will continue as they are. To create stability in our relationships, we must recognize the issues and establish boundaries for them. Scripture provides a frame of reference for viewing issues of power and control. They are components of the authority given to humankind and are referenced in the first chapter of Genesis:

²⁷ So God created man in his own image, in the image of God he created him; male and female created he them.

²⁸ And God blessed them, and God said unto them, Be fruitful, and multiply, and replenish the earth, and subdue it: and have dominion over the fish of the sea, and over the fowl of the air, and over every living thing that moveth upon the earth.

—GENESIS 1:27–28 (KJV)

This authority, our capacity to think, choose, feel, and love, and truth empower us. These properties and other senses permit us to adapt to our environment and define how we will function in it. They also provide the frame of reference out of which we can act responsibly and effectively in all aspects of our lives. There is no magic wand to create wholesome relationships where respect, caring, and balance are valued and nurtured. They require work, and building them takes time—some relationships longer than others.

SIX

I Don't Think He Loves Me Anymore

DEPRESSION AND ANXIETY DROVE SOFT-SPOKEN, SIXTY-TWO-year-old Maggie into therapy. Her marriage to the man of her dreams was falling apart. They had met at a church social and married twenty-six years ago. He was everything Maggie ever wanted in a man and she had loved him very much. She still did, but the way he had acted in the past year made her feel that he didn't love her anymore. Maggie was the second wife of the sixty-eight-year-old, college-educated, retired insurance broker. There were no children from their union. His two daughters from a previous marriage had been reared by their mother and stepfather. Limited contact with their father through the years extended into adulthood. They were not close to him or Maggie.

Beautiful, trim Maggie dressed stylishly. Her regular beauty and exercise routines showed in her appearance. She thanked me for the compliments on her physical fitness and told me how at age twenty-three, she changed her beauty habits after reading Lena Horne's comments on preparing for old age in an *Ebony* magazine article.

"As bad as I feel, I still try to look good," Maggie acknowledged. "I'm losing weight now because I can't always eat. I've lost my appetite but I force myself to eat a little something. I don't sleep too well, either. When I started crying all the time, I knew I needed to talk to someone. I was in one of your workshops and decided to call you."

"I'm glad you came."

"I am, too. I'm miserable but I keep up a front. I still cook, clean, and make our home comfortable for him even though he acts like he doesn't appreciate it. The atmosphere around the house isn't hostile; he's just indifferent toward me. It doesn't seem to matter whether I'm there or not. He eats his meals at home but goes into his office after and stays there until I have gone to bed."

Maggie's golden face flushed. "He hasn't touched me in a year." She paused to regroup. "I don't talk to him or even speak to him because I don't know what to say." Her voice lowered to a whisper. "I don't know what to say anymore. He tells me when he is going out—every Thursday for the past six months—but he doesn't say where he's going or when he is coming back. I guess I'm too old and boring for him now."

Throughout the first session, Maggie tearfully aired her frustration and helplessness at failed attempts to revive the marriage. It was difficult for her to talk to her husband. He answered her questions but did not respond when she tried to engage him in conversation. When asked, he accompanied her to social functions but no longer attended the church services that were once a part of their life together.

Ashamed to let anyone know about their deteriorating marital situation, Maggie withdrew from friends and spent more time alone. She was relieved to talk confidentially since previously she had chosen not to share her story. I encouraged Maggie to continue sharing in a journal and include what she wanted to happen in therapy. She ignored my suggestion to ask her husband to attend one or more future sessions to hear his input.

During the next few sessions, Maggie told more about her life and marital relationship. She and her high school sweetheart entered junior college immediately after graduation. Both had completed a year when he was drafted and killed in the war in Vietnam. Devastated by the news and unable to concentrate, Maggie abandoned school at the beginning of her second year. Three months later, she moved from her hometown to work as an administrative assistant for the law firm from which she eventually retired. Her social life centered on the church, as it had at home with her parents and two sisters.

Maggie was thirty-five years old when she began dating her future husband. Divorced for almost three years, he'd finally agreed to attend the church's singles-ministry social after weeks of beckoning by a male cousin. Maggie was there. The weekly gatherings were her main social outlet. He'd talked to her throughout the social and also become a regular. Their friendship grew into romance and marriage after eighteen months.

On the whole, their marriage was good. Maggie and her

husband were mutually devoted. They spent a great deal of time together at church and went out for dinner regularly. At home, they watched television and spent quiet times together reading and listening to music. He complimented her appearance and efforts to make him and their home comfortable. Maggie's infertility was not an issue for either of them. She was satisfied just to be married to him.

A significant portion of Maggie's life involved church and charity work. Through the years, she ran errands, grocery shopped, fed, and visited the sick and elderly members in her community. Maggie's husband often drove her around and waited to make sure she was safe.

Maggie missed the good times. Her weak excuses that he was tired or busy somewhat eased her anxiety but she worried about their future together. We ruled out poor health and finances as factors. He, too, was physically fit from daily exercise and proper diet. Regular physical examinations confirmed his good health. Investments, real estate property, and retirement pensions made him financially sound.

At the fifth session, Maggie shared unspoken fears. She suspected marital infidelity but was reluctant to raise the issue. The pain and fear of losing her husband overwhelmed her. Deep inside, she believed he had only been attracted to her beauty and style and wondered how much her aging affected his present behavior toward her. As an aside, Maggie remarked there was just so much that a person could do with looks because time always took a toll.

Though concerned about the effects of aging, Maggie did

not appear to be obsessed with her looks. Nor did she view herself as interesting. She compensated for this apparent lack of confidence by doing things for others. Maggie took care of everybody. I experienced her as a pleasant, considerate woman who attended conscientiously to details in all aspects of her life and performed tasks diligently.

"It seems like you spend a lot of time taking care of other people," I probed to refocus Maggie's attention onto her behavior.

"Yes, I do. But you know, it really isn't a problem for me. It's something I've always done. My mother used to tell me, *Don't be so concerned with yourself. Make sure you do something for other people or you'll end up selfish and alone.*"

"How did those messages play out in your life?"

"Well, I'm quiet. I never had too much to say so I volunteered to do things. At school, at work, at church. Like I said before, it's not a problem for me."

"In what ways were you appreciated?"

"Appreciated?" Maggie paused for a memory search. "Sometimes, uh, most of the time, I guess I was taken for granted. People like for you to wait on them and when you do it a lot, they expect it from you. That's just the way it is."

"How do you want appreciation shown to you?"

"Me? I haven't thought too much about that. I don't need a big fuss over me. Saying thank you. Maybe a card or flowers once in a while. I like flowers. Oh yes, including me. Including me in the activities, not just as an afterthought."

"In what ways did you let the people in your life know what you needed from them? How did you let your husband know?"

Maggie hunched and released her shoulders. "I guess I haven't. I assumed they would just know. My husband should know. We've been together a long time."

"How would he know? He can read your mind?"

Maggie thought for a while and answered, "I've never considered that either. You act a certain way around the people close to you and you don't think that you have to tell them to do right."

"It doesn't work that way, does it?"

"No, but it's not fair."

"I wish I could make things right for you but I don't have the power to do it. You do. You can't change your husband but you can change his responses to you. The principle applies to everyone else, too."

Maggie looked at me, puzzled, declaring that she had already done just about everything and it hadn't made a difference. Her statement frustrated me because the language suggested an acceptance of defeat. I asked her to think through my statement to determine what it said to her and how she could apply it to her life. Maggie did not have questions at the end of our session and left promptly.

At our next meeting, she launched into reflections on our previous discussion. "I thought a lot on what you said about changing my husband's responses to me. I prayed about it, too. I do a lot of praying." She paused. "To me, it means, I can take care of other people but I have to take care of myself, too. I have to do the changing—be responsible for my own happiness."

A frown creased Maggie's brow. "That's hard because I have always linked my happiness with my husband. I want him to love me again. God knows I do. I hate to think that it might not happen but I'm trying to come to terms with it. It's hard, though."

"You've done a good job taking care of yourself physically and spiritually. Maybe we can look at ways to take care of yourself emotionally."

"Yeah. But I don't know how."

"Let's begin by defining what you want for yourself."

In order of importance, Maggie wanted to restore her husband's interest in her, get rid of her anxiety, and feel better about herself. The prospect of living alone frightened her and she wanted to be prepared if it happened. We reviewed the goals to see if they could be achieved. Restoring her husband's interest was beyond our control because only he could change his behavior. The others were possible because she could do them.

Maggie's concern that she had to become a monster to gain respect eased as she began to understand that change does not have to be negative and punitive. She could remain the same person who assessed and responded to situations differently. Self-acceptance meant consideration of her needs as she prepared to respond to others. Habitually, Maggie acted on others' needs before her own needs to be liked and accepted.

The self-preservation idea bothered Maggie. She immediately recalled the childhood admonition that it is selfish to consider yourself and questioned if this wasn't so. It is selfishness when you consider only yourself all the time, I explained. Love and care for ourselves is one side of the scale. Love and care for others is the corresponding side. Too much emphasis on either side creates imbalance.

The statements made sense but felt odd to Maggie. She would write about them to understand their messages and meaning to her life. I warned that she was establishing her own personal comfort zone, not playing a game to win her husband's affection. The results of her efforts could be favorable or unfavorable. He might respond either way. In any case, clear motives and honesty were crucial steps in redefining her life with or without her husband. Otherwise, she would deceive herself and be open to more hurt and despair.

THE PROBES INTO MAGGIE'S PERSONAL AND MARITAL SIT-uation stimulated her to look for areas to introduce change. She eliminated busywork from her daily routine and added some of the things she most enjoyed but never did. Since spiritual commitment was a priority, she strengthened it with daily prayer, meditation, and writing.

In her journal, now a companion, Maggie uncovered buried emotions and clarified further changes to be made in her life. Taking care of herself physically was already established. She thought about a second career but wondered if it was too late. More possibilities occurred. She wanted to restore neglected friendships and learn to talk more directly and effectively.

Planning engaged Maggie's time and energy productively and eased more of her anxiety about the situations over which she had no control. Assigned readings of scriptural stories and passages and books by women with similar life situations helped her see how they coped and reduced her feeling of isolation.

As Maggie connected with her personal power, she became stronger and more decisive. She continued courteous behavior at home and resumed daily greetings whether her husband responded or not. Her peaceful acts modeled noncombative behavior and released Maggie to be courteous and agreeable as she was normally. To do otherwise would have hurt her more than him. She chose to go on with life, despite her pain. Maggie grieved the loss of her husband's affection and the marriage relationship. Grief and pain were natural reactions to her loss.

I explained to Maggie that each of us reacts to pain differently. In failed relationships especially, some of us try to deny our pain. Others try to hurry it along so they can move on to their next relationship. Still others stubbornly hold on to pain and use it to justify inappropriate behavior. None of these tactics works. Pain exists as a part of our human package, and there isn't a lot we can do about the feeling. It's gone when it's gone.

Maggie's pain was trapped energy. Acknowledging her pain began the process of releasing it. Only then could the space be available for more satisfying emotions. From experience, I knew that Maggie's pain would eventually lessen, then disappear, if she truly wanted it to go. If not, the nurtured pain would spawn resentment and bitterness, and grow large enough to destroy her.

Over the next several weeks, Maggie continued working through her grief and feelings of helplessness. Blame and guilt intruded to undermine her confidence. Eliminating them was a challenge. Week after week she strove to replace each with favorable thoughts and emotions. Daily affirmations helped in this cause.

With her world falling apart and hurting, Maggie felt compelled to regain her personal power, even though her husband might reject the new behavior. She took the risk to heal. Recognizing alternatives and choosing those that empowered her became immediate tasks. Cultivating language to accompany her new behavior followed.

Maggie practiced improving her communication skills. First, she identified how her husband's behavior made her feel and rehearsed by saying the statements aloud while alone. ("It's not easy when you ignore me. I feel rejected and alone. I'm humiliated when you talk down to me.") Sharing the impact of his behavior on her provided opportunities for him to act differently, if he so chose.

Secondly, Maggie identified suggestions for improving the situation in question. ("It's not easy when you ignore me. I feel rejected and alone. I could handle it a lot better if you would say something. I'm humiliated when you talk down to me. I would appreciate if you stop and think before you say something that degrades me.")

Prudent use of Maggie's feedback could improve their relationship. It would show that he listened and wanted to cooperate. If he ignored the information, Maggie faced staying in the relationship as it was defined or acting to improve her condition. They both faced choices.

We discussed why there wasn't a need to argue and fight about the information. As adults, both had the right to live and choose in their best interest. However, neither had the right to choose for the other, particularly when the impact of the choice was negative, destructive, and each had already been told what was needed from the other.

The first time, Maggie shared her feelings after dinner at the table. She told him that ignoring her belittled and emotionally shut her out; that talking to him was like talking to a stone wall. She was too nervous to add anything else. He didn't look at her while she talked but he listened. Maggie felt his eyes on her as she left the room.

The second time, she acknowledged their deteriorating relationship and asked for him to comment on it, out of respect for the time they had spent together. This was new behavior for Maggie. Before, she had grieved silently. Though still in pain, she continued the new behavior but avoided confrontations.

Her husband noticed the changes but initially did not respond to them. Gradually, he returned her greetings but sat through their meals without conversation. At one mealtime, Maggie was strong enough to say she loved him and wanted a better relationship. Still no response from him. Maggie said a decision needed to be made about their relationship. She wanted it to be made together, but if not, she would be forced to decide alone. Again, her husband listened but did not comment. Although the unknown outcome frightened Maggie, she felt better about herself with the changes in her behavior. She wasn't as anxious and passive, and recognized that her self-esteem had grown.

In our continued exploration of lifestyle changes, Maggie

discovered that her finances permitted living alone comfortably but not extravagantly. Good health insurance, annuities, and retirement compensation were in place. Travel hadn't been a priority and still wasn't. Maggie wanted most to complete the requirements for her associate's degree in the arts. She had always wanted to return to school but had never mentioned her desire. She longed for the knowledge and confidence from college to help establish her lifetime interest, a home-based millinery (hat-making) business.

Quality-of-life issues and adjustments to a different lifestyle surfaced as Maggie became more confident. Prominent among them was whether or not she was content to live with her husband's indifference and be miserable. She was not. Maggie returned to school without her husband's knowledge.

A semester passed before her husband reacted to the change in her routine. Maggie was preoccupied and out of the house more frequently. He was home more and watched her transformation but didn't say anything. After several class conflicts prevented Maggie from preparing dinner on time, her husband confronted her. He asked if she was seeing another man and, before she could speak, firmly added he would not stand for it. He accused Maggie of acting like she didn't love him anymore.

It was the first time he had talked meaningfully to Maggie since her change in attitude and behavior. Glad that he was talking but surprised at his conclusions, Maggie listened willingly to his concerns. Her preoccupation and movements disturbed him and he pressed her for an explanation as to what was happening in her life.

For several days they discussed their relationship, lifestyle, retirement, and aging. During their talks, Maggie revealed her return to college to earn a degree. Her husband received the news coolly but exhaled on learning that her new interest was school and not another man.

In our meeting, Maggie talked about his efforts to reconcile. She still loved her spouse but her attitude toward him had changed. Where she once devoted the largest portion of her life to pleasing him, she now included her own interests and desires. New definitions and activity filled the vacancy created by his alienation. She wasn't the same as before and didn't want to be. Contacts at school and affirmations of Maggie's intelligence and abilities in classes strengthened her.

Self-evaluation forced her husband to face his mortality and marital infidelity with a younger woman. Maggie's changes helped him to see that he highly valued their life together. Apologies and requests for forgiveness followed. His love for Maggie had never wavered; the fear of aging overtook him.

They resumed their married life together with her changes and his renewed attention. Maggie earned her degree and accepted her husband's experience and financial support to help establish a home-based business. Her growth astounded them both. She used long-hidden talents and interacted with others more expressively. The changes improved her self-esteem and provided new direction to her life.

Toward the end of our contracted time together, Maggie telephoned to see if she could bring in her husband. Initially, the therapy/crazy association intimidated Maggie too much to invite him. She didn't want her husband to think she was crazy for seeing a therapist. However, she had come far enough along in healing to let him know what was going on. As a therapist, I was very curious to learn about his reasons for attending. I reserved the last fifteen minutes of a session for him to join us.

They were a stunning couple, both medium height, trim, and muscular. His graying temples and conservative dress gave off a distinguished look. As we met, a brilliant smile lit his handsome face. He admitted to curiosity about the person and place that had stimulated Maggie to change. Irritated initially, he now appreciated the new dimension to their relationship. Maggie gazed admiringly at him as he spoke and I answered several questions about the therapy process before ending the session.

In concluding sessions, Maggie and I reviewed themes, issues, goals, and accomplishments. She acknowledged clutching her pain until deciding to do something about it. Therapy provided a safe, supportive, nonjudgmental environment for her to work through grief, clarify life issues, and choose wisely to make her remaining years meaningful. Though painful, she reconnected with her personal power and improved her life situation.

Maggie was glad her relationship had survived. The mutual caring and respect they retained in their marriage provided a foundation on which they continued to build. Acknowledging his wrongdoing opened the door for Maggie to forgive him. Forgiveness served as a strong element for their healing.

Not all troubled relationships end with reconciliation. Mutual caring and respect are necessary for a relationship to survive. When one party does the work for both, the scale is weighted on one side and there is no balance. A successful relationship requires the cooperation of both parties. All relationships require work.

Women who surrender their identity in relationships typically experience lower self-esteem. Women who choose to stay in unbalanced, unhappy situations are usually miserable and blind to honorable options open to them. None of us was created to live in misery. We were all born for a purpose. Living meaningfully is to discover that purpose. Identifying our unique gifts are clues to our purpose in life. Using our gifts helps us to experience richer and more satisfying lives.

Choice remains the ultimate option. Achieving a comfortable state in life is possible if we choose to make it happen. Clarity includes knowing what we can and cannot do. When we are clear, we can choose wisely. Choice is selecting what to do. Action is doing. Together they give us power to define and manage our lives.

SEVEN

Too Ashamed to Tell

QUIET AND RESERVED AVA IS A FORTY-SEVEN-YEAR-OLD woman who looks ten years younger. At five feet, eleven inches and 135 pounds, she is in good health. Ava does not smoke or drink. She holds a master's degree and is a personnel specialist in the federal service. Her parents are deceased; she has no siblings or children. From day one, Ava's spouse of seventeen years abused her. She recently separated from him after he almost killed her.

Ava wore carefully applied bronze makeup to conceal the occasional face bruises and dark circles under her eyes, though the effect didn't go unnoticed. Her manager suspected that she was a battered wife, and recommended she get counseling.

Ava struggled with the suggestion because counseling was a new and uncertain idea but finally she decided to go. After she said little or nothing during the three sessions provided by her agency's Employee Assistance Program (EAP), the counselor gave her my name. Ava entered therapy with me only after canceling five appointments. She always called with reasons such as: "My manager is having an impromptu meeting and I have to reschedule." "I put my car in the shop and it's still not ready." "My head is hurting so bad I need to go to sleep." She was too ashamed to tell her story. Yet over the next two months, Ava described the events of her life in endless detail.

Fifteen minutes early each week, Ava waited patiently for her sessions to begin. She honored the time limit for the sessions but continued to speak even as she walked through the doorway. Once started, she couldn't stop talking.

Ava moved from her isolated, rural hometown to the city for better employment opportunities after high school graduation. She secured a clerk-typist position and advanced to secretary a year later. Impressed with Ava's intelligence, demeanor, and good work habits, her agency provided a career development plan for on-the-job training and tuition subsidy that spanned twelve years.

Over the first eight years while working, Ava earned her college degree. Life was fine. She lived with relatives, dated, attended social functions, and enjoyed college and work. After graduation Ava was promoted to a professional position. Four years later, she earned a master's degree in personnel management.

Ava is the first and only member of her family to attend and graduate from college, but her parents didn't live to see it. Both died during her pursuit of a bachelor's degree: first her father; three years later, her mother. During their lifetime, her parents barely managed on their meager salaries as unskilled workers. There was never enough money to live comfortably, and Ava's father used a little more than his share to buy alcohol. Although his drinking caused many of the ongoing family battles, they stayed together through the turmoil.

When Ava saw her parents fight or when her father thought she neglected an assigned task, he lashed out verbally at her. Talking about him usually brought an excuse for his behavior. She was used to him or knew he didn't mean any harm. That's just his way and at least he didn't beat her.

A high value on worship motivated Ava's mother to attend weekly Sunday school and church services with Ava at her side. There and at home, Ava watched her meditate and pray quietly. She savored her mother's company, even though they spent their times together mostly silently. Talking was not her mother's strong point, and she rarely answered questions. Ava learned to accept the silence, the faraway gaze, and standard reply that things would work out in the end with the Lord making a way.

At a party several months after receiving her master's degree, Ava met a midlevel government manager and entered a six-week whirlwind courtship with him. Impressed with the attention and the gifts he lavished on her, she accepted his marriage proposal without ample knowledge of him, his past, or his family.

Early in the marriage, Ava yielded to her spouse's demand to manage the family's finances himself and turned over her bi-weekly paycheck. Their combined income represented an avenue to the financial security she craved, even though she had no voice in managing the money. He selected and maintained all major purchases. She bought miscellaneous household and personal items, groceries, and clothes from the one-third of her salary allotted to her.

Her husband's need for control spread to other areas. Accusations of infidelity with coworkers surfaced immediately after they married. One missed telephone call from him at work summoned charges of sleeping around and demands to know the man's or woman's identity. Neither gender escaped his indictment. Daily, he questioned her whereabouts and lunch partners. A barrage of derogatory names about Ava and her character followed his probes and persisted throughout breakfast and dinner preparation and serving.

Initially, Ava tried to neutralize his accusations with affectionate gestures and pampering. When she succeeded, he apologized, expressing his love and how he missed being away from her. These episodes ended in lovemaking and, often, he left money the next day with instructions to buy something nice for herself. This routine continued with periodic quiet days but, overall, his behavior worsened.

Ava alternated between silence and arguments in responding to her husband. No response on one of his bad days invited bedlam. She could expect to be awakened by name calling along with one or a combination of middle-of-the-night antics: door slams; the radio, television, or CD-player volume on loud; books dropped to the floor; or a shaken bed from his side-to-side flips throughout the night. It took a toll: Ava suffered through the night and went to work tired the next morning.

The abuse began with occasional pushing and shoving when her husband was displeased and expanded to punches and hair pulling as his anger escalated. Ava's miscarriages during their second and fourth years together followed acts of anger. The first time, she was three months pregnant when his shove upset her balance and plummeted her down their duplex apartment stairs. She miscarried the second time under similar circumstances, six months after moving into their new home.

His acts grew more intense over the next four years. The ridicule and scorn dealt at every opportunity undermined her confidence. Unending scolds and insults during friends' visits alienated them. Embarrassed, Ava no longer invited anyone to their home. Gradually, she withdrew from all social activity except church.

A few times, Ava's husband carried out his threat to taunt her at church. Shortly after she sat down, he slithered into the pew beside her and whispered complaints and criticisms throughout the service. Usually, he left before the service ended but resumed the harassment when he saw her again.

Home life became torturous. The nightly loud noises increased and broke Ava's rest. To compensate, she napped before her husband came home. The occasional glass of wine to help Ava sleep during the weekend stopped when her husband placed bottles of wine in her bedroom, bathroom, and the kitchen—places where she couldn't miss seeing them.

Their sexual life moved from sex-on-demand to occasional-sex to no-sex. He moved himself and his belongings to a basement room and they lived apart. Ava never knew when she would see him. Sometimes he left the house at dawn and returned either in the wee hours or not at all. Other times he left early in the morning, returned shortly, and stalked Ava until she left for work or church.

He ignored the meals Ava continued to cook. Instead, he purchased groceries, separated them from the existing ones, cooked, and ate by himself. After trying unsuccessfully to satisfy him, she stopped.

With growing frustration, Ava pondered her nine years of unhappiness and status as a working woman without enough money but continued in the marriage for another eight years, hoping to make things better. Most of the time, she was broke. The tide changed when Ava accidentally found a savings account statement in her husband's name only. Stunned and hurt, she opened an automatic-deposit bank account to reclaim her salary.

Enraged at the change, his temper erupted. Ava endured the onslaughts but never knew how much more she could stand. The filth that sometimes came out of his mouth was worse than a punch in the face. Her husband alternated the assaults with extended periods in which he said nothing at all.

Work and the workplace were havens. Conscientious and dedicated, Ava dug into her job to escape. She was a familiar figure in her pastel knit suits and dresses—stylish and well groomed despite problems at home. A very short haircut eliminated her husband's hair-pulling episodes.

Tale after tale, Ava related incidents that wore her down emotionally. Their darkened house triggered her anxiety whenever she came home alone. Too many times, the lights revealed booby traps to startle and unnerve her. One evening after arriving home from a church activity, Ava found sharpened pencils sticking out from the wall baseboards when she switched on the living room lights. Another time, the lights didn't come on because the bulbs had been loosened.

When dressing for work or church, it did not surprise Ava to find only one earring from a favorite pair or to discover that a new dress had disappeared. Once in a while, she found the missing earring tucked under a sofa cushion or in the rear of the linen closet.

The greeting cards he gave to Ava on special occasions sent degrading and obscene messages. His gifts added insult. They might have been an old pair of her shoes; new shoes two sizes too big or small; or a used household appliance, such as an iron, a toaster, or transistor radio. All were beautifully wrapped.

Growing up, holidays and birthdays were always special times, but Ava's attempts to make them pleasant and festive during her marriage were forever thwarted. Her husband saw to it. Still, Ava set the table and decorated for special days even though she spent them alone. Preparing for holidays engaged her.

On the night before Thanksgiving, Ava's husband was particularly hostile and agitated. As she prepared the holiday dinner, he sat with folded arms in the dining room and sullenly studied her movements through the French doors that separated the rooms.

One door was slightly ajar when Ava attempted to open it wider with the movement of her hand on a pane. The other hand held a flower vase for the table. Abruptly, her husband jumped up and shut the door with such force that Ava's hand smashed through the pane. He rapidly reopened the door so that the broken pane scraped back across her hand in a second movement that severely cut her fingers and hand. She bled profusely. The injury was a nightmare come true.

Her husband fled to another part of the house and removed the hook from the telephone cradle to prevent her from calling for help. On hearing her loud frantic screams, he replaced the telephone hook. Ava called the police. She screamed to stay conscious, feeling she would surely bleed to death if she blacked out before help arrived.

Both rescue squad and police responded to her call. Broken glass marked the spot of the attack. Trails of blood and bloody footprints on the carpeted floors outlined Ava's movements. One of the rescue firemen asked incredulously if there had been a massacre. They took Ava to the hospital. Police arrested her spouse. Though released from jail the next day, a court-issued order for protection prevented him from returning to the house.

The hospital summoned a hand surgeon for reconstructive surgery on Ava's arrival. The countless deep cuts and near amputation of her third finger required an eight-day hospital stay and six weeks of leave of absence from work. For months after, she received physical therapy to regain the use of her hand.

The separation from her husband provided the peace and solitude to evaluate her situation and determine her next moves. Ava initiated steps to adjust to her new single status. The court system, a support group, and her family network proved to be valuable resources. The court system extended the order for protection, which prevented intrusions from her husband and supplied information on her legal rights and recourse as a battered wife. From a hospital support group, she learned more about abuse and resources to help abused women.

Ava reached out to her extended family, telling them details about the injury, and asking for their support while she rebuilt her life. Both biological and church families rallied around Ava during her recuperation and subsequent court proceedings.

FOR SEVENTEEN YEARS, AVA HAD ENDURED EMOTIONAL, physical, and sexual abuse in silence. It was important for her to understand why she tolerated the negative behavior so she would not repeat it in any future relationships. We looked at the sources of her abuse and how they were reinforced in her interactions with her husband. Her parents' lifestyle and values provided clues.

Ava learned passivity from her mother. The family battles intimidated and frightened them both. Ava transferred this fear and coping style to a spouse who displayed behavior similar to her father. Her fear was legitimate. The frequency and severity of her husband's emotional and physical assaults led her to believe that one day he would kill her.

We explored further her reasons for staying in the unhappy, abusive marriage. Financial security ranked highest. The amount of their combined income represented success, particularly in light of her family's financial status. Her husband used Ava's insecurity about money to manipulate her. She reclaimed her salary, but the constant warnings from him that she could not live solely on it threatened and confined Ava.

A tradition of no divorce in her immediate and extended families was another reason Ava offered for staying in the marriage. The subliminal message from her parents' model was to stay in the marriage regardless of the interpersonal dynamics. To leave signaled personal failure and inability to carry on the family heritage. The message was that marriage was forever—at any cost.

During the course of therapy, we worked to eliminate fear, manage stress, build self-esteem, and develop new options. Before Ava met her husband, she had a fairly active social life and good relationships with relatives, coworkers, and church members. He had willfully alienated family and friends. The isolation and silence about her situation imprisoned her at home and shut out people who could have helped her escape.

Studying her reactions and defense patterns helped us to identify the fear, insecurity, and passivity that had operated throughout her life and relate them to her current stressful situation.

The process of eliminating Ava's fear began with naming it. She probed inside to understand why she was afraid. Ava dreaded being poor and unable to live decently. She felt her husband would someday kill her and cover it up successfully. Also, she thought no one would believe her if she described what was happening in their marriage. Fear overwhelmed and paralyzed Ava. Uncertainty over what would happen next kept her anxious and intimidated. Sadness enveloped her because she felt trapped.

Asking herself and completing statements about why she was afraid, at least ten different times, helped to put her in touch with her fear—for example, "I am afraid because I think he's going to murder me and get away with it." Saying the statements aloud continued the naming process and engaged her hearing and speaking senses. In her journal, Ava recorded the statements as well, to provide more definition. Naming the fears and emotions defused them. When you can name fear, you have something concrete and can work to get rid of it.

Ava felt powerless. She gave away her power by surrendering her capacity to choose how she would function in the relationship with her husband. She knew no other way to act. Eliminating fear required Ava's awareness of her power to change.

To change, Ava had to understand and accept the notion that something can be done about anything. The process followed a formula: Identify what is needed, where to get it, who will do it, and when it will be done. It changed Ava's attitude. Action followed.

Prayer and meditation helped Ava to manage the stress from her marriage. Worship and church attendance had sustained Ava's mother as they now did Ava. Since Scripture was consistent with her religious frame of reference and tradition, we used it throughout therapy for guidance, comfort, and to restore Ava's self-esteem.

Psalm 139 was our starting point. I call it the self-esteem psalm because it stimulates thoughts about our source, power, beauty, and responsibility. Assigned as homework, Ava read and studied the psalm by answering the following questions:

- What is the Scripture asking of me?

- What is it saying to me?

- What does it mean to me and my life today?
- How will I use the information in my life?

Homework assignments provided a structured way for Ava to continue working on the problems presented in therapy. Reading and writing in her journal promoted emotional healing. Both actions served to release tension and to address issues. Writing helped to define boundaries for future same-sex and opposite-sex relationships:

- I will expect the best for myself.
- I will put myself first, sometimes.
- I will ask for help when I need it.
- I will not tolerate unfair treatment.
- I will say no as many times as I need to.
- I will honor my convictions and opinion.
- I will take care of myself.

Reading about battered women eased her feelings of isolation. Eighteen months of depositions, hearings, attempts by her husband to evict Ava from the home, and exorbitant lawyers' fees preceded her divorce decree. Then Ava finally began a peaceful life with new definitions of how she would function in relationships. The thought of being in her husband's presence still triggered twinges of anxiety. Deep-breathing exercises and stretching helped her to relax. The support group she joined increased her confidence and social network. It allowed Ava to see that other women were dealing with the same problems. It eased the feelings of isolation about the things that had happened to her. The self-disclosures cleared a path to work through issues that consumed her energy. Redirecting the energy led to greater personal definition, stress management, and personal growth.

In preparing for termination, we discussed the need for her to continue to work on herself. Taking care of yourself is not selfish—it is a way to become strong. Ava made tapes of favorite music to play during deep breathing, luxury baths, and exercise. Ava's spiritual life of prayer, meditation, and church attendance maintained her sanity and eased her isolation throughout her ordeals.

The outline for Ava's formal stress management plan provided guidelines for self-care.

Stress Management Plan: Taking Care of Myself

1. What stresses do I need to watch for this week? List them.
2. (a) How will I care for my physical self? Generate as many options as I can.
   (b) Of the options listed, select one or two to be carried out during the week.
3. When will I begin the option selected to care for my physical self?
4. (a) How will I care for my mental self? Generate as many options as I can.
   (b) Of the options listed, select one or two to be carried out during the week.

5. When will I begin the option selected to care for my mental self?

6. (a) How will I care for my spiritual self? Generate as many options as I can.

    (b) Of the options listed, select one or two to be carried out during the week.

7. When will I begin the option selected to care for my spiritual self?

Each week, Ava completed a stress management plan unless the previous week's carried over. She continued this process until it became natural to include physical, emotional, and spiritual dimensions in self-care.

AVA'S STORY IS BOTH SAD AND TYPICAL OF MANY ABUSED women's lives. Fear of her husband and the accompanying anxiety and depression took their toll. The abuse violated her safety needs, lowered her self-esteem, caused emotional pain, and injured her severely.

Ava's spouse used emotional, physical, and sexual abuse to get her to do what he wanted. His behavior was designed to gain and retain control in the relationship through humiliation, and through creating insecurity about Ava's self-worth and ability to escape further mistreatment.

In a follow-up interview with Ava a year after therapy, she shared some reflections on her marriage.

"As I looked back, I realized that I stayed in the marriage too long because I thought I couldn't make it on my own. Because of the psychological browbeating and the trauma, I thought I couldn't. That's a bad feeling. I lost my confidence.

"I went through periods of depression and anxiety. When he was in a good mood, I was glad but anxious, waiting to see when he would blow up. When he did, I was depressed. I was up and down like a seesaw.

"You have to take responsibility for your own happiness. If you don't, you are vulnerable to manipulation. That is what he did. I allowed him to manipulate me. I gave him my power.

"I'm doing better now that I've gained my self-esteem. With the support of my family and other support, I gained my confidence and found that I can live within myself. I'm satisfied within myself. I realized that I have the capacity to live a happy life without him. The bottom line is, be satisfied with yourself; build your life around yourself.

"My support was crucial. Don't try to do it by yourself. You have to tell what is happening in your life. Someone will believe you. Isolation can cripple beyond repair—you can be killed or end up in a mental institution. The isolation and trying to work out your situation alone are the abuser's strongest points. Nobody knows what is happening to you so he has his way. What was done to me was done when I was alone."

"What would you have me say to other abused women?"

"Bruises don't always show. Go to the hospital or your doctor for documentation. A purple light will clearly show the bruises. Oh yes, make sure you talk to the policeman writing the report when they come to your home or go later to add your input.

Sometimes you even have to check to make sure they filed a police report. In retrospect, I realized that my husband talked to the one who was writing it. When I read the report, it was slanted toward what my husband said. I looked back at the incident and saw that I was hysterical when I called the police and I wasn't around when they took the report. Later, I went to the police station and added my version of what happened so it would also be in the record.

"My other advice is to reevaluate yourself and your potential. Set a goal of your own and pursue it. I was living my life within his boundaries—his life, his actions, and everything he said, thought, and did. When I took a good look at my life, I realized that I didn't have one. I regrouped."

"Regrouped? How do you mean?"

"Have a philosophy of life based on what makes you happy. Everything was contingent on what he wanted; what made him happy. In other words, I didn't have a life. Discover what your purpose is in life and do it well. If you don't know, go somewhere and find out."

"Are you still afraid of your husband?"

"No. I would probably try to kill him if he bothered me now. I get angry when I think of how I allowed him to intimidate and abuse me all those years. I know better now."

"Did he stop harassing you?"

"Yes he did. He never thought that I would follow through in the courts like I did and divorce him. When it sank in that I wasn't playing and I wasn't afraid of him anymore, he left me alone."

"Are you in a relationship?"

"No. I can't handle one right now. It's interesting, though. I must have some kind of sign on me that attracts certain kinds of men because I see my ex-husband's traits in the two who are pursuing me. I need more work on strengthening me before I allow another man in my life. That's what I'm doing now. I am making new definitions. Pampering me. Taking care of myself."

"Are you afraid of men now?"

"I think trust is the real issue with me now. It will probably take some time for me to let another man in my space. Well, I guess that is fear. Yes, maybe I am still a little afraid of men."

"In what ways have you used the boundaries you established?"

"I am taking better care of myself, and that includes making sure that I am first sometimes and not always last. Speaking up for myself is one of my biggest steps, instead of letting people take advantage of me. That was hard for me but I'm getting better at it. Oh yes—the more I say no, the more I *can* say no."

Ava drew on her inner strength to survive. Attention to her spiritual, physical, and mental self helped her to maintain balance. Each dimension supplied energy to counteract the forces of an unhealthy home environment and circumstances.

EIGHT

Stolen Innocence

CHILDHOOD SHOULD BE A TIME OF INNOCENCE, A TIME TO be carefree and happy. Not so for girls like Pam, however, who were robbed of their virginity and carried the secret into adulthood.

Pam called for an appointment on the recommendation of a friend whom I'd seen in therapy a year earlier. Neatly dressed in a jogging outfit and smiling, she bounced into the room. Taking the lead, Pam extended her hand to shake mine, introduced herself, and greeted me. She plopped on the sofa without my prompting, and quickly surveyed the room with her peripheral vision before speaking freely, but superficially, about herself, family, and jobs.

"I'm a twenty-six-year-old college graduate and don't even have a job. My sister does. She has her own apartment. I live with my parents. They work in the government—they didn't go to college."

Pam's plump, ringless fingers swept over her short-cropped natural hair. "My mother pushed me to go to college. 'Get-your-degree-so-you-can-support-yourself-and-be-independent,' " Pam mocked in a singsong tone. "Huh. That's not the problem. I can get a job, I just can't keep one." Pam smiled broadly and waited for me to respond. When I didn't, she continued her introduction by telling me bits and pieces about herself.

Since graduation from college, Pam had held a series of temporary clerical jobs on which she stayed three months or less then quit. With sharp computer-programming and interviewing skills, getting jobs was easy. Pam talked a good game and looked attractive in the tailored suits she reserved for interviews. Vibrant and attentive, she charmed her way into jobs.

Efficiency and cheer radiated from Pam during the month or so it took to learn the people and office procedures; then, once the routine was established, her interest waned. The cheerfulness at work dissolved into distraction and restlessness at home. A depressed mood enveloped Pam and she overate. In three and a half months, fast foods and late-night refrigerator raids expanded her five-foot-two frame from 110 to 155 pounds.

"Why are you here?" I asked.

Throwing her head back, she feigned a light, casual tone. "Oh, it's time for me to check in again. I'm tired all the time for no reason. I don't sleep well, but you can see that I eat well. When I do get a good night's sleep, I still feel weighted down—like somebody's standing on my shoulders."

"Who have you seen about this?"

"A psychiatrist."

"Tell me about your visits."

"Which one? I've seen a few."

I waited for Pam to continue.

"Seven, in fact. I've seen seven psychiatrists. All of them White men." Pam smiled.

"How long did you see them?"

"Off and on over the past ten years."

"Ten years?" A red flag went up in my head. *She didn't show this on her intake form. Ten years and still searching. What's going on here?*

Pam answered. "I get upset a lot. I cry. I scream. I fall out when I'm upset. I go to the psychiatrist. I talk to him until I feel better. I leave when he pokes too deep. I never stay longer than three months." From under her breath she added, "On my jobs either."

"Tell me what you talked about."

"The same things mostly. My childhood. My parents, their fighting. My sister, my life."

"What did you learn?"

"Oh—that we don't have it together. We're not the model family. My mom is screwed up; so is my dad—but I already knew this before I saw a psychiatrist. I have to take responsibility for myself and rework my dysfunction. Same soup reheated. I understand our family dynamics and what they represent for me but I still hurt." Pam looked directly into my eyes. "Help me with my pain."

As the session unfolded, I learned that Pam came from a household in which her father had abused her mother. Fights were frequent and often so violent that her mother's injuries required hospitalization—once for two weeks. Her return home to the same fights after discharge frustrated Pam. Afraid that she would end up like her mother, Pam pleaded for a way to escape.

As we sat quietly for a few minutes, my inner voice spoke to me: *I know she's been traumatized but she's been over all of it with the psychiatrists. What's Pam not telling?* The question plagued me. I asked for more about her life at home.

Pam was twice hospitalized in a psychiatric ward with hysteria over her parents' violent fights. Both times they treated and released her after three days. To escape the arguments and fighting, she and her sister retreated to their paternal grandparents' home. Pam refused their offer to stay permanently, preferring to wait until her parents' tempers cooled. Though weary from the battles, she felt obligated to be home to support her mother emotionally.

Pam's sister remained with their grandparents to complete high school, earn a license in cosmetology, and begin work as a beautician. She moved to an apartment and limits her contacts with the family.

I asked, "What else do you want to tell me about you?"

"Nothing." Pam dismissed me.

"Do you keep a journal?"

"No." She wrinkled her brow.

"I'd like for you to begin one. It will help you to ventilate some of the things inside. Write about our session. Write about what you want to happen in therapy, whether you continue with me or not."

Pam had no questions for me. I asked her to get a physical exam to rule out any condition that might be related to her fatigue and lack of energy. She stood, telling me on her way out that she would schedule her next weekly appointment with my receptionist. From her behavior in the session, I saw that she was accustomed to therapy, but trust was an issue.

At the following session, Pam again bounced in bubbling and took the lead. She sat facing me with crossed legs propped on the sofa. Today she wore a matching cap to complete her colorful jogging outfit with Nike tennis shoes.

Pam drilled me. "I didn't have questions before, now I do. Are you married?"

"Yes."

"How long?"

"My business." We both laughed.

"Any children?"

"Three," I said, adding, "where is this going? Do you want to use your time asking questions about me?"

"Okay, okay, okay. Where do you want me to go?"

"More about why you are here."

Pam plunged into a recital. Her beautiful, chocolate face and dazzling smile attracted men. Liaisons with the ones she chose lasted for short periods—one or two months—after which she ended them or they did, saying she was strange. Pam questioned what she was doing wrong when after easy starts, the men became possessive, jealous, and violent. The behavior baffled then frightened Pam when she realized the men were like her father. Smiling again, she dismissed it as too much work to stay in a relationship.

"What happens next?" I asked.

"I get in a slump and I can't pull myself out of it. That's when I start crying and can't stop. I cry anytime but I haven't been in a relationship for a while now. I haven't been up to it."

"How did you handle this before now?"

"With the meds. They didn't take the pain away but I felt better. They made me sleep. He, my psychiatrist, explained that I had symptoms of depression."

For the remainder of the hour, Pam focused on depression— her accumulated knowledge from experience, years of contact with psychiatrists, and reading. She was on stage, showing off her knowledge of depression and how it affected people.

I was Pam's audience today. I listened, knowing that she would do anything to dodge the pain she was in. Pam admonished my glance at the clock with a sharp reminder that her time was not up, smiled again, and continued her lecture. I still didn't say anything, but I felt a creeping irritation. She was pushing my patience buttons.

As we discussed our future together in therapy at our next meeting, Pam told me of her decision to stick with therapy.

"Stick?" I questioned. "How did you reach this decision?"

"The vibes are right and you're a sister. Anyway, I told you, I'm tired. I'm tired of running."

"Running?"

"Yes, *running.*" Pam smiled broadly as she squeezed the words out through clenched teeth. "Are you always gonna do that to me?" I raised my brows quizzically. Smiling and speaking more evenly, she continued. "Question me with one word?"

"Probably. I already know what I mean by the words, I want to understand what you mean by them. Our meanings may not be the same."

Pam did not respond.

"So what are you talking about?" I asked.

"Pain in my life. Pain in my childhood. I've been running a long time. Running from pain."

Pam retold the stories of her parents fighting and her reaction to it. Sensing her caution and need to establish a comfort level, I listened.

THROUGHOUT THE NEXT FEW SESSIONS, PAM BOUNCED cheerfully into the office, taking the lead and rehashing—as she reminded me—content explored in sessions with previous therapists. Speech punctuated with psychiatric jargon flowed from Pam. Her smiles glowed like neon lights, even when she spoke about painful topics. No journal either. She didn't get around to it. Pam was not ready to deal with further truth about herself, but she faithfully appeared and rigidly observed the time limits for each session. I remained mostly passive to convey my acceptance, but she was wearing me out.

Bounce and cheer were missing in the seventh session. Pam

was somber. With hands locked behind her head, she talked more about her liaisons with men, describing repeated happy beginnings and disastrous endings. I intervened by calling attention to the smiles that didn't match the topics. Momentarily, Pam stared at me before admitting laughingly that it was just something she did. "I've always done it."

"Oh? And people let you get away with it?"

Pam's smile faded as she unlocked her hands. "I guess so."

I had to puncture the armor to go deeper. The shield that covered her pain also prevented us from moving to its source. Smiles hid Pam's emotional pain. Smiles also brought compliments that counteracted bad feelings about herself. Pam needed to dismantle her armor and replace it with confidence, positive attitudes, and wise choices. Suitable actions would follow.

"For now, I just want you to be aware of the behavior. You have to be true to yourself, Pam. It's really the only way to find peace."

Pam sat silently for a long moment with no expression on her face. Her deep sigh broke the silence. "My smiles are rewarded. They always have been. People said isn't she pretty and pleasant. Teachers favored me because I smiled." Pam mimicked a southern drawl. "They said, 'He-ah is Miz Son-shine.' I smile and I'm treated better."

"How much work is it?"

"Whew." Pam blew a stream of air. "You can't imagine. I've smiled through some pretty rough times. I still do."

" 'We wear the mask that grins and lies.' "

"Oh. Paul Laurence Dunbar . . . 'With torn and bleeding hearts we smile.' " She paused and sighed again. "You know that's the truth. You really can't tell what's behind smiles."

Pam lowered her voice. "I have a problem with intimacy. You wouldn't think so. I'm afraid of it. I have a lot of trouble with sexual intimacy. Deep down, I never really want to be touched. It makes me feel dirty. Sometimes, when it's going on, I feel vulnerable. Something that happened to me comes back in my mind and makes me cringe and freeze. Other times I just bite my lip or grit my teeth until it's over. Then I start crying and can't stop."

I leaned forward. "What happened, Pam?"

"It happened a long time ago."

"Go on. Tell me about it."

Haltingly, Pam began. "My mother has six sisters. She sent me down south to her mother's house in the summer. Two of my aunts live with my grandmother and both of them have a son. My grandfather died before I was born." Teardrops trickled down Pam's cheeks. "My cousin used to mess with me. Putting his hands and mouth where they weren't supposed to be—and you know what else. I hated going there because he was there. Sometimes, I'd be in the house. Sometimes, he got me when I was playing outside."

The tears became steady streams as Pam told me about the visits. From age eight until she was twelve years old, the younger of Pam's male cousins sexually abused her. He was seventeen years old when the violations began. The older cousin was twenty-five and rarely home.

The abusive cousin was home with Pam when she did not accompany her grandmother on errands. Her aunts, described as weekend drunks, were usually home but paid little attention to most things happening around the house. They only yelled for him to stop bothering Pam when she cried out to them. Neither asked what he was doing nor why she cried so much. They called her a crybaby.

Pam whispered, "I know you're going to ask me why I didn't tell somebody. I was scared and I didn't think that they would believe me. My cousin tried to act like he was so innocent but someone should've been watching him."

He intimidated Pam from the beginning, threatening to kill her mother and sister if she told anyone what he did. Periodic smacks supported his intentions, as did threats to claim that she'd seduced him. *No-one-will-believe-me* drummed in her ears. Young, innocent Pam took his threats seriously. Pam's parents dismissed her pleas to stay home, saying the visits to her grandmother were good for her. They never questioned why Pam consistently did not want to go—they never knew that the cousin terrified her.

A tiny frown creased Pam's brow. She could no longer speak. Glimmering unshed tears leaked out of the corner of my own eyes. I moved closer, placed Pam's hands in mine, and held them until she regained her composure.

The disclosure shook me. Pam was the first of the young women I treated who broke the silence on their sexual abuse as children. I thought about it long after she left. Still later that evening, questions raced through my mind. Had that ever happened to my sisters? To my friends? I'd never heard any of them say anything about it. I never heard anyone say anything about sexual abuse.

When Pam missed her next two weekly appointments, I remembered her dropout patterns with former therapists and her *running* response to pain. Nevertheless, the break allowed me to reflect more on our time together. Pam's disclosure was a wake-up call. It left me thinking a lot about how the abuse affected her behavior and troubled her life. I wondered how many women were living with pain from the same secret.

The answering machine sounded with her cheery message when I called the second week to tell Pam her slot was still open. She did not return my call but reappeared for her appointment on the third week.

Pam began the session by explaining her absence. "I never told anybody about my abuse. My family, my therapists, no one. I had a real bad time after I told you about my cousin. I felt like the world was going to crash down around me and I would be alone, standing in the middle of trash. All I wanted to do was run. But you know, there's something really funny about it. Sometimes my thoughts, my heart, and my head are going at full speed but outside, I feel like I'm moving in slow motion."

"Racing in quicksand."

"Yeah. Yes. You know, this stuff is awful. I mean, it has a horrible effect on you. I try to front but that's all it is, a front. My self-esteem is in the toilet." Pam shook her head side to side repeatedly. "You wouldn't believe some of the things. I feel bad inside. I don't even look at myself in the mirror. I look past myself. I can't stand to see my reflection in the mirror or look at my body. I shower and dress without lights because I feel ugly. I don't like that person I see." Pam's eyes filled and overflowed with tears.

"What's happening now?"

"Pain. I hurt. Before, when I tried to talk about it, the words stuck in my throat. My heart beat fast and my head felt light. Now I can't stop the words even when I try to hold back. Feels like they'll explode in my throat if I don't let them out."

A floodgate sprang open and Pam poured out the details of her abusive experiences: the penetration and pain; the sights, sounds, and smells; the humiliation, fear, and guilt; the disgust. Once, in swift movements, one of her aunt's male drinking partners had brushed his lips across her forehead and his hand across her arm and breasts before she ran from him. Distressing memories of the abuse intruded whenever she was touched.

Pam's symptoms indicated post-traumatic stress disorder: the intrusive memories that affect her intimacy; the repulsion she experiences in intimate situations; outbursts of anger; difficulty in concentrating associated with staying on jobs; sleep disturbances; and the associated symptoms of depression. The trauma was the childhood sexual abuse, the stress of which was compounded from years of hiding it.

Pam stayed at home before and after her parents' fights to try to reduce her father's attacks on her mother. This protectiveness toward her mother may well be related to the protection Pam needed but did not receive as an abused child.

Abuse leaves scars. Residual effects of intimidation, fear, hurt, and guilt move into adult relationships and influence a woman's interpersonal behavior. Talking about the abuse eased some of the isolation Pam felt and began her healing. Disclosure and ventilation are the first steps toward healing. She had to tell what happened and talk about it to release the energy entrapped with her secret. She had to challenge the negative emotions that resided within her mind, body, and spirit.

OVER THE NEXT TWO MONTHS, WE EXAMINED THE ABUSE, pain, and their connection to her guilt, shame, and lowered self-esteem, to facilitate healing. The guilt emerged from feelings that she had done something wrong, disappointment, and fear of punishment. I confirmed the fear of her cousin's reprisals as legitimate and intimidating enough to sustain her silence.

Eliminating guilt began with understanding she was not responsible for what happened. Within this context, we explored the significance of touch and how it was an important part of her beginning life. Mother's cuddles and affectionate hugs made her feel secure and established blueprints for safe touching. She experienced the difference from her cousin's violations, which threatened and demeaned her. As a child, Pam did not know how to say no effectively, or to make herself heard to the inattentive adults around her.

Low self-esteem and shame carry underlying unworthiness: *If he did this to me, then there must be something wrong with me;* and *I deserve to be mistreated because there is something inherently wrong with me.* Pam's negative self-evaluations, festering inside as secrets, fed on themselves and were hard to replace. Week after week, we chipped away at them with additional speaking, reading, writing, and mirror assignments. Yet forgiveness for herself and permission to move freely in the present and future remained obstacles.

I recommended some affirmations, from which Pam selected those to speak each day. First she listened for the message in the affirmation, then wrote about it in her journal. Speaking, reading, and writing them engaged her senses and provided new, positive language to replace the old.

- "I will praise thee; for I am fearfully and wonderfully made: marvelous are thy works; and that my soul knoweth right well." (Psalms 139:14, KJV)

- "I forgive myself. I didn't know any better."

- "I am learning to take care of the physical, mental, and spiritual dimensions of myself."

- "I forgive myself. I don't have to stay in the past. I can be in the present."

- "Death and life are in the power of the tongue: and they who love it shall eat the fruit thereof." (Proverbs 18:21, KJV)

- "I didn't know any better in the past. I'm learning to make better choices."

- "I give myself permission to take care of myself today. It's all right to do so."

- "I look forward to a positive future."

- "I will have a blessed day. I will take time to do something that really makes me happy."

- "I will not cringe or utter disclaimers when I am complimented."

- "I will compliment the appearance and abilities of others and accept compliments graciously when they are given to me."

For assigned reading, Pam indulged her love of poetry with favorites by Paul Laurence Dunbar and the beautiful collection of poems in the Psalms, newly found to her. She also liked the wise sayings in Proverbs. Finally, Pam agreed to regular journal writing for release and rebuilding.

A few weeks earlier, we had discussed mirror exercises and used them to look at her face, see physical beauty, and build self-esteem. With Pam the first time, I held her hand as she stood before an office mirror. Her eyes instinctively snapped closed. Three or four times, Pam glanced alternately at her image and away until she moved from the mirror's path to escape the reflection's magnetized pull on her tears. Looking was painful. Each week after that, a look in the mirror became a ritual.

The homework assignments to look in the mirror each day were carried out first with glances, then looks, and finally with stares. Concurrently, each week I took a Polaroid photograph of Pam. She refused to look at them initially but I continued until she became comfortable with her image. The latter photographs began her assignment to build an album with pictures that reflected a new attitude.

Pam's disclosures and heightened awareness made her mad. The anger was for her stolen innocence. "Why me?" was the expression of her anger. The unfairness of it all aroused rage, and she directed her resentment toward the most accessible persons, her parents. At home, she acted out her anger with hysterical crying, screaming episodes, and irritability.

I confirmed her anger as a normal response to grief and suggested that we redirect the anger to use it constructively. We discussed how telling her family about the abuse would be a way to ease some of her anger. The energy required to keep her secrets fed on itself and, with no escape, would continue to fuel her anger.

Another month passed before Pam told her parents. Lumps in her throat at first thwarted attempts to explain her behavior. Yet Pam realized that her continued healing required telling her parents about the abuse. One evening she asked them to listen to something important they needed to hear. The revelations hurt and saddened her mother. Spousal battles had blinded her to Pam's suffering. Enraged and ranting, her father vowed to kill the young man. After the initial shock of hearing about the abuse, Pam and her mother convinced him to join in a discussion of steps to be taken.

Two days later, with parental presence, support, and encouragement, Pam told other family members about the violations. Her maternal grandmother believed her immediately. Her aunts went wild, vehemently denying that it could have happened. For six weeks, Pam and her parents persisted, demanding accountability and ignoring the aunts' suggestion to drop the subject.

Tension within the family grew. The aunts stopped talking to Pam and her parents. Her grandmother intervened. Over the next several months, she convened two family meetings and required the aunts to either participate in resolving the matter or move out of her house. In the meetings, her grandmother addressed Pam's disclosure of sexual abuse, the family's reaction to it, and the family's role in resolving the tension. Pam's desire for her cousin to acknowledge his abuse against her did not happen. On hearing that she had told about him, he left the home. Subsequently, he was arrested and incarcerated for drug trafficking.

Still, the family's support helped Pam's healing process. They believed and rallied around her. She no longer suffered alone. She no longer accepted the blame for the violations to her as an innocent child. Pam understood the impact of abuse on her emotions and self-esteem—violations that made her feel dirty, unloved, and unworthy of love.

Releasing her stored emotions gave Pam the energy and space to rebuild her self-esteem and her life. The process required a safe, supportive environment for Pam to talk. Her abuse was a severe emotional injury that had been left untreated and had not healed properly. Talking reopened the wound but, in doing so, also exposed the infections of guilt, disappointment, and anger that required attention. For each, she first acknowledged that the abuse was not her fault then examined emotional alternatives by answering the questions: What power do I have to change my feelings of guilt, disappointment, and anger? What else can I do to help myself?

Asking buried questions also helped Pam to dissipate her anger. The journey to shed the guilt began when she accepted that it was normal and realistic to expect protection from the adults in her family. Learning that her symptoms revealed post-traumatic stress informed Pam that she was not alone in her feelings and reactions to the abuse. She came to understand how past events had influenced her present behavior with men.

Pam adopted language that prompted her to speak positively about herself and her life. She turned negative statements about herself into positive and forward-moving statements. For example, when Pam began a statement with "I will never be able to . . . ," she changed it to "Up to this point I did not . . . but I am discovering ways to . . ." Changing the direction of the statement from negative to positive did not require denial that a bad situation existed. It meant that she approached the situation with an attitude that she could do something about it. She could act in her favor.

Truth freed Pam. Telling the truth provided a new model to follow and allowed her to dump the trash that had accumulated inside from her negative experiences. When we identify the truth in any of our situations, we connect with our essence and are strengthened by it. Truth empowers us.

Pam initiated reconciliation with her sister, who agreed to let Pam move in temporarily while she reestablished her life. Pam also took small steps to establish relationships with males by defining boundaries for herself and them:

- I have the right to take care of me.

- I have the right to protect my body and treat it with dignity and respect.

- I have the right to say no as many times as I need to.

- I have the right to participate in decisions involving me.

- I have the right to be alone, even when others want to be with me.

- I have the right to walk away from a bad situation.

- I have the right to determine what is best for me.

- I have the right to expect the best for me.

She recommended family therapy to her parents and no longer accepted responsibility for her mother's unhappiness.

Pam and I worked together for thirteen months. In a letter to me three months after her therapy ended, she talked about her self-esteem:

As long as I can remember, I didn't look at myself in the mirror or identify with who I am. I lived in total darkness. Recently, the doors to that darkness were unlocked and for the first time in my life, I was introduced to a part of my being that I never knew. For once, I could look in the mirror without running or seeing total darkness. When I looked as the darkness faded away, I was a face with a pair of eyes, a mouth, nose, lips, eyebrows, and lashes. All of it was amazing to me. I never knew these things existed. It was just amazing to me! For the first time in my life, I met me face-to-face. There was a smile—soft and sweet—smiling at me. There were these deep and beautiful eyes looking at me. I quietly said to myself, I like her. My lips. Oh! I was blushing at my lips. I was amazed at who I saw. It was me.

This amazing experience made me realize that I was once blind but now I see through my eyes, God has lifted me. There was a time that I never knew of this person that I am now.

PERIODICALLY, PAM CALLS TO LET ME KNOW HOW SHE IS doing. The last time we spoke, she was working steadily as a computer systems analyst. She still lives with her sister, goes out occasionally with a mixed group of friends, and has lost ten pounds.

NINE

Behind Closed Doors

AMY IS THIRTY-SIX YEARS OLD, TALL AND STATUESQUE, with jet-black hair worn straight in a blunt cut. Exceptionally attractive, she is a divorced attorney with a twenty-year-old daughter who'd lived with her ex-husband from the age of two, when Amy had yielded what she thought would be temporary custody. Amy is the only child of college-educated, upwardly mobile, professional parents. Both are accountants.

After watching a televised discussion of domestic violence in which I appeared as a panelist, Amy called and fired off a number of questions about therapy and me. She made an appointment two weeks later when my name surfaced as one of three therapists given by her insurance company.

Curt and guarded in our first meeting, Amy plunged into questions about therapy before I offered introductory remarks and asked why she'd come. "How long will it take? Are reports written? Who has access to the information? Why is there a co-pay?"

I responded. "Therapy is a restoration process to help us function more effectively. The time it takes varies. It depends on the severity of the condition and your willingness to work in the process. Minimal progress notes are taken and they are confidential. Co-pay is your portion of the total fee-for-service."

Poised in a black Ellen Tracy mini-skirted suit with matching shoes and accessories, Amy sat expressionlessly. Her manicured fingernails were barely visible beneath her folded arms. As the long pause stretched, I saw that she was not ready to speak and didn't push her. It was the beginning stage of building our relationship and I yielded the space she needed to be comfortable. I continued speaking to fill in the time.

"The longer we live, the more our inner space becomes filled with information and experiences from our lives. Too much of it causes forgetting, acting out, or other physical and psychological symptoms. I call it 'data overload.' If our spaces are filled with more bad than good, we are weighted down with negative thoughts and activity. Imprisoned, they stagnate, decay, and prevent us from cultivating our potential. They cause disorder in our lives."

I chose not to answer Amy's continued barrage of questions about therapy and disorders but instead offered office pamphlets for further information. When I suggested that she might want to use the time differently, her body stiffened.

Amy still wasn't ready to talk about herself. She restarted with alternating questions and comments about women who came for therapy, psychologists portrayed on television, and more. For thirty-five minutes, Amy filled the fifty-minute session with superficial, rambling talk. I suggested that discussing her reasons for entering therapy now would give me a better sense of how to help.

There was a brief silence as Amy looked off into space. "I think I might need some help. That program on domestic violence stirred a lot of emotions in me. I've always been able to manage them but I've been a little too touchy lately." She stopped talking. Her almond-shaped eyes gazed far beyond the room.

At my nudge to go on, Amy turned to me and stared absently a moment before focusing. "Irritability keeps me from being as productive as I can be. It's—uh—sort of always been there. It's more pronounced now, since I saw the show. Parts of it set me off—the part about abuse. The show was about emotional, physical, and sexual abuse in families."

Amy had started to unwind but it was time to go. I asked her to continue sharing in a journal and include why she came and what she wanted to happen in therapy.

At the following session, Amy was more relaxed but still a bit edgy. She launched into a discussion of the time-consuming nature of her work and the added pressures related to her status as the sole African American attorney in a small corporate firm. Aloud to herself, she wondered if she would someday make partner, then expounded on how the company leaders arbitrarily changed their rules midstream and the energy required to manage the changes.

I heard more about her as she continued. Anxious and depressed, Amy did not sleep well. A nonsmoker, she drank three to five glasses of wine a week, took no prescription or other drugs, and worked out three times a week at the gym. Visibly tense when I asked what her mother and father were like, she said nothing. I noted her reaction and moved to problems she had experienced as a child at home and school. Her jaw tightened, and again she didn't respond. I had touched nerves and backed off. I didn't want to scare her away.

On her third visit, Amy arrived fifteen minutes early and stood in the waiting room until I ushered her into the office. She acknowledged her reaction to my questions about her parents and thanked me for not pushing. After a long, deep sigh, Amy invaded the wall of secrecy surrounding her childhood, family, and sexual molestation by her father.

"I was a model child, they tell me, and my mother had me enrolled in dancing, music, skating, and every kind of class you can name when I was little. You see, on the outside, we looked like the perfect family but at home, it wasn't so good. Not at all. At first, we did things as a family but after a while, my dad was cold and indifferent to my mom.

"He was still nice to me but he stopped eating most of his meals with us and moved out of their bedroom. Mom didn't say anything about what was going on. She acted like everything was all right but I noticed that she started to drink and go on a lot of business trips. That left me damned unprotected! The bastard started fondling me when I was eleven years old!"

"When did it stop?"

"At fifteen. I fought him. I scratched him up and took my ass out of there. I've never been back. I never told my mom. I don't think she would have believed me if I had. One time, when she came back from a trip, I told her she needed to leave him. She never responded. She didn't question me or anything."

Amy's father did not penetrate her but inappropriately touched, rubbed, or kissed her in the genital and breast areas on many occasions when they were alone. Other parts of Amy's story revealed that after the molestation began, her behavior at school and home changed drastically. Her grades fell; she withdrew from extracurricular activity and skipped school. After too many absences for promotion to the next level, she dropped out. With her adopted peer group, she drank, used drugs, and engaged in promiscuous sex. She did anything to escape her unhappiness.

Amy shifted in her seat several times before continuing her story. "I took my family as long as I could then I ran away to live with my boyfriend. I was fifteen; he was twenty-five. He thought I was older. I got pregnant, married him, and later found that I couldn't stand him. I couldn't stand his touching me or saying anything that sounded like my father. I split and went to live with my grandmother in another state. She sent me to college and paid for my graduate education."

"How long did you stay together with your husband?"

"A little over two years."

"What happened while you were there?"

"It was a trip. He was okay. I was too young. I earned my GED but it was rough trying to be a wife, care for a baby, and go to school. I realized my head wasn't right for raising a child. I still wanted to go to school—that was drilled into me by my parents.

"My grandmother was very supportive when I talked about going back. She was going to keep the baby but my ex made such a stink, I gave him temporary custody. He claimed he was taking me to court for desertion and charges that I was an unfit mother—dragging all kinds of shit in. I didn't need it." In a quick movement, Amy sat erect and folded both arms. "I didn't know it at the time but I could have countered him with statutory rape. I was only fifteen when I got pregnant."

Over the next ten weeks, we worked through the impact of the abuse. Amy hurt deeply. Depression and flashbacks of the molestation were constant companions. Images from the violations renewed her vulnerability. At other times, memories of the defilement intruded on her dreams and taunted her. Guilt confused and tormented her, especially when she remembered that some of his touches had aroused her. She didn't dare speak of that; didn't know what it meant. Amy had said nothing of what had happened to her, until now.

Her abuse bred fear of intimacy and abandonment, as well as distrust. These traits remained in her psyche and influenced her expectations in relationships. Suspicions about honesty and fidelity surfaced as well as apprehensions about desertion, betrayal, and hurt. Both produced the dilemma of how to respond in wholesome ways and maintain self-esteem in relationships while fears and distrust were present and raw. When she became suspicious and apprehensive of the men in her life, they often interpreted her behavior as inborn negativity, put-downs, or both. Their battles began without valid understanding of the underlying reasons for them.

Angry and argumentative, Amy released her emotions in same-sex and opposite-sex relationships. On examining them further,

she revealed her contempt for males who resembled her father and elements of punishment in her behavior toward them.
Verbally and sometimes physically, she assaulted those who confronted her about her out-of-control behavior. Caught simulta-
neously loving and hating her father, Amy rode an emotional roller
coaster. The memories of violations by the man she'd loved and
on whom she'd depended caused excruciating pain. The betrayal
spawned feelings of abandonment, rejection, and worthlessness.

With female acquaintances, Amy searched constantly for signs
of betrayal. When she felt slighted or interpreted an action as an
attempt to demean her, she ended all forms of communication
abruptly and avoided the offender's presence. After a two-month
to two-year period, she resumed contact and acted as if nothing
ever happened. The pattern wore thin on her friends. The remaining few who'd waded with her through the years of ups and downs
were now distancing themselves. She was lonelier than ever.

At Amy's request, we extended our sessions beyond the initial
ten-week contract period to continue working on her challenges. As she released pent-up emotions, we examined what
they represented and how they motivated her to act as she did.

Trust and abandonment were issues. Amy distrusted deeply
and questioned the motives of everyone who tried to befriend
her. She was never certain if expressions of caring for her were
real. Her grandmother was the only person with whom she felt
safe and supported. With everyone else, she expected obligation
and waited for their requests for payoffs.

We explored, further, the inconsistencies modeled by her
parents and the behavior she'd carried into her adult coping style.

Together she saw them as materialistic and superficial. She saw her father, the primary male role model in her life, as immoral. Publicly, he paraded as a respectable figure; privately, he was the opposite. Mixed feelings about him extended to males who sought a relationship with her. She assumed that their intentions were negative and invariably lashed out at them.

Anger and hurt lingered from what Amy considered her mother's abandonment and insensitivity to her need for protection. She viewed her mother's frequent business trips as escapes from the family's problems. Anger and hurt lingered from her mother's failure to recognize the acting out as a cry for help. Amy wanted her mother to ask what was happening, but she never did. Her mother's silence and her father's sexual violation negated the protector roles Amy expected and needed as a child. She wept on recalling how she'd felt unloved by her mother.

Amy didn't feel loved and didn't love. While she knew her behavior affected friends, her need for protection overshadowed everything else.

"With my friends," she said, explaining her instability, "I was either dealing with the betrayal in my family or the struggles with my husband. I couldn't concentrate on relationships outside of them. It was too taxing. I was too overwhelmed and insecure. Thinking back, I guess I was lucky to have any friends—the aces that hung with me through the years. It seems like I was always dealing with two sets of people: my real friends and the pretenders. The pretenders perpetrated frauds—acted like friends when they weren't. Too much insincerity and competition. I didn't trust them and they didn't trust me but we still did things together.

Weird, isn't it? Real friends accepted me no matter how I acted. They never hassled me. I've probably lost them by now. I'm going to do better. I've got to do better."

With friends, Amy repeated the pattern modeled by her mother: say nothing and run when unable to cope. We persisted in search of the truth. To create a new model and choose wisely now and in the future, Amy needed clarity on how what happened had affected her life, and why.

By the fourth month, we began to focus on the issues Amy could resolve and the behavior she could change. Throughout, she flashed into anger and wept. Her anger was a challenge because she had nourished it for many years. We acknowledged anger as an authentic response but also a destructive one when uncontrolled. Amy vented some of it in preparation and delivery as an attorney. In relationships, however, her anger barreled like a loose cannonball over anyone in her path.

In identifying ways to dispel her anger, we concentrated on her learning to be honest with herself. Each of Amy's traumatic life events carried emotions and truth. Being honest involved getting in touch with the truth and acting on it, no matter how painful. Amy examined areas that troubled her by answering a series of questions in her journal.

- What is plaguing me?
- What is the truth?
- How do I feel about this event (person, situation)?
- What have I done with my feelings?

- How has the event affected my life?

- What have I done about it?

- What have I overlooked?

- What will I do about it?

- What else do I need to consider?

- What do I have control over?

- How will I exercise my control?

- In what ways will I express my awareness?

Pain still radiated from feelings of alienation from her mother. Amy's journal entries were among her attempts to confront it:

I can't seem to get it together with my mom. We were kind of close when I was little. I got a lot of stuff and she gave me money. I couldn't understand why she was so blind. How could she not see or sense what was going on? How come she never asked me any questions? When I think about it, I feel this coldness around me and I never want to be around her anymore. But when I feel deserted, I have this achy feeling around my heart and in the pit of my stomach and want to see her. Then I get mad.

The truth? My dad molested me. I didn't tell my mom. I assumed she would know. I'm not happy with the way things are with us but I don't know what to do. Okay, Amy, the truth. Yes I do. I'm taking off my blinders. I've asked for help to straighten out my stuff. Truth: I haven't forgiven my mother but I love her.

What have I done with my feelings? Nothing with the achy ones. It's easier to deal with my anger. I can mow down anyone who gets in my way. I work it out in the gym and with work. Maybe, wine helps with the achiness. It keeps me from thinking too much and helps me sleep. I haven't consciously considered my feelings. The pain is just there. How do you tell somebody stuff like that about your mother—your parents? Hell, I don't want anyone in my business like that. All they'll do is use it against me. I have to be strong to survive.

Affected my life? How has this shit affected my life? Seems like I'm my mother's child. I guess I'm doing what she did: running away from problems and drinking to escape pain. Wonder if my daughter will be the same way? But I haven't been around her. Maybe she'll have it better since she wasn't around me. I don't know. I've got to leave this shit alone right now.

What have I done? I'm in therapy. For me that's a big, big step 'cause that's not our thing. But I couldn't handle it by myself anymore. I've got to move to another level.

Overlooked? I don't know. I guess I overlooked that there are consequences for whatever we do. We get fallout from what we do, no matter whether the fallout is good or bad. I'm trying to deal with that now. I guess I overlooked that my mom was going through something, too. A bad time, too. I don't know. It boggles my mind to even think about all of this. I'm out of here.

In her sessions and journal, Amy labored for more than a month to come to terms with her feelings and express them. She asked and answered the self-directed questions several times before recognizing her power to act. Once achieved, she planned to invite her mother to a session to talk. Amy prepared for the meeting by writing letters to her mother and reading them aloud in the sessions.

Her mother agreed to come readily when Amy invited her. She did not know about the abuse beforehand because Amy had not disclosed it to anyone prior to entering therapy. In my brief talk with her before their meeting, I conveyed Amy's wish to establish a closer relationship. With painful issues haunting her life, Amy felt less threatened with me present to facilitate. I explained that my role was to help them talk nondefensively and interact as much as possible. She was anxious but glad to be included. Amy's mother also hurt deeply from their estrangement.

In their first joint session, Amy and her mother faced each other in adjacent chairs at opposite ends of the sofa. Amy sat erect with folded arms; her mother leaned forward slightly with hands resting in her lap. They sat quietly and looked alternately at the floor and at each other for a long time before they both began to cry. The nonverbal communication between them was intense. I watched.

Amy's mother stood, walked hesitantly toward Amy with her arms extended. Amy stood. Their crying escalated as they embraced and held each other. Amy broke the silence to express relief at their meeting. Sitting together on the sofa, they spent most of the time communicating nonverbally: weeping, holding hands, and embracing. Amy told about the abuse; her mother apologized;

they were silent. When the time was up, both asked for more sessions together to work on their relationship.

In the two joint sessions that followed, they talked more about their lives: the abuse, the child, the questions, the issues, and their feelings for each other.

From Amy: "Did you suspect that anything was wrong? Why didn't you ask if anything was wrong? Why did you ignore the signs and changes you saw? Why did you stop loving me?"

From Amy's mother: "Yes, I suspected something was wrong—another woman in his life but not you, Amy. I saw and didn't see the signs. Our marriage was bad and he treated me badly. I was so caught up in my own misery that I couldn't see anything else. It was hard for me to cope with anything. My father intimidated me as a child and a brutal beating by him during my early teens broke my spirit. I'm sorry I wasn't stronger for you.

"Your father pushed me to fight for your child but at the time, I suspected it was his way to keep me tied down. Caring for the child required triple duty again: working, being a wife, and parenting a young child. I needed too much love myself to nurture the child. The thought of a grandchild depressed and entrapped me. Deep down, I felt my marriage would not survive and I needed to be free to restructure my life.

"You see, I also married against my parents' wishes. When the relationship soured, I was too embarrassed to tell about the trouble—the hell I was catching. Amy, I loved you the best I knew how and I love you now. I'm sorry about what happened to you and your daughter."

As Amy's mother continued her story, I saw that ineffectual interpersonal behavioral patterns had been passed down through the generations. Amy's maternal grandmother was also passive and withdrew when her husband (Amy's grandfather) acted irresponsibly toward the family. Her grandmother ran from trouble and drank to escape. Amy's mother characterized herself and her own mother as weak and afraid. The pattern passed from mother to daughter, but she had wanted a better way for Amy. She apologized again.

Amy had not maintained contact with her father. He'd stopped trying to contact her when she'd refused to accept his occasional telephone calls through the years. Anxiety stirred during the few times she'd seen him, and she moved away to avoid him. Amy did not want to reconcile.

Her father left the home and her parents divorced after a five-year separation. Amy's mother entered therapy to resolve some of her own issues and to learn to create better results in her life.

Amy and her mother are working on their relationship. Amy also wrote to her own daughter. The child had been nurtured by her father, stepmother, paternal grandparents, and their extended families, and lives on her own near them. Amy hopes to move toward a relationship with her daughter, from whom she is alienated, if possible, but she hasn't heard anything, as of yet.

Amy displayed symptoms of post-traumatic stress disorder. Many of the women in therapy who were sexually and emotionally abused as children experienced the same symptoms. The abuse compromised their safety and changed their lives. Situations that once seemed safe were no longer so.

Post-traumatic stress is an emotional response to a shocking, painful, extraordinary event. It involves reliving the traumatic event and the distress associated with it through dreams, nightmares, or flashbacks. The trauma may occur with a single individual, as with Amy in childhood sexual abuse, or in groups of people, as in war. Natural disasters such as volcano eruptions and floods; accidents like fires and automobile or airplane collisions; and violent acts, like shootings, rape, and the Twin Towers disaster, can all trigger post-traumatic stress after three or more months have passed.

Amy's therapy began with telling her story of molestation, hurt, pain, acting out, desolation, and abandonment. Releasing the sealed feelings began the healing process. In her journal, Amy wrote about her emotions and the questions she'd never asked. Writing permitted her to ventilate, clarify, and later discuss her feelings with her mother. Reading assigned works by women with similar experiences helped Amy as she identified her issues and worked through them.

A stress management plan included daily quiet time alone for meditation, short walks, and luxury baths to reduce anxiety. She used weekly structured exercises to plan how to care for her physical, mental, and spiritual needs. With the support from therapy and her own network of family and friends, Amy continued to heal by developing new ways to respond.

I CALLED AMY A YEAR LATER TO SEE HOW SHE WAS DOING. Periodically, she and her mother telephone, visit, and dine out at restaurants. Their relationship is still strained but they are trying to work it out. Amy's intense involvement in the law practice consumes most of her time. While she regrets that her daughter has chosen not to be in her life at this time, Amy understands that the decision is a consequence of her own earlier choices. Participation in a support group following therapy has helped Amy through uneasy times.

TEN

Advice and Reflections

BLACK WOMEN LIVE WITH THE REALITIES OF A SEXIST, RACIST environment and learn to cope with the restrictions and discriminatory practices that have always been present in our society. By example through the generations, Black women have shown the will to survive through the most adverse and painful situations. During those times, we perfected the art of taking care of others. Taking care of ourselves needs to become a priority now, however, because of its implication for our physical, mental, and spiritual health. This means learning to move beyond survival modes and present new models for ourselves and our daughters to follow.

Silence masks pain and becomes a way of life when disclosure is too threatening or dangerous. Pain drove the women into therapy to confront the issues that hurt them. Removing the cloaks of silence eased their pain and released the energy trapped with their secrets. Liberated inner space allowed them to redefine how to function in more satisfying ways.

Symptoms of Abuse

As I reviewed the comments made by the abused women in therapy, some statements appeared so frequently that I listed them. The checklist items are samples of behavior and do not include all of the acts that can be committed. They may help women who are questioning their partner's negative behavior toward them. Similar questions may be found in works on physical, emotional, and sexual abuse.

EMOTIONAL ABUSE

- Constant accusations about practically everything.
- Animosity toward my friends and behaving nasty and rude while they are visiting.
- Bad-mouthing me and my family.
- Telling me how I can't do anything right. I can't do things like his mother or grandmother did them.
- Criticizing everything in public and private.
- Threatening to hurt my family and friends.
- Constantly telling me I am nothing; nobody.
- Put-down remarks, name calling, and yelling profanity.
- Taking me out then ignoring me, or refusing to take me out.
- Refusing to help financially.
- Throwing away or hiding shoes, dresses, and jewelry.
- Deliberately messing up the kitchen, sink, or house after they have been cleaned.

– Using my best towels to wash the car.

– Digging in the yard with my best silver.

– Cohabitating with his mistress/other women.

– Withholding affection, appreciation, or approval to
   punish me.

– Threatening to kill himself if he does not get what he
   wants from me.

– Blaming me for everything that goes wrong in
   his life.

– Posting nasty notes around the house.

– Moving the mail, magazines, other articles where I
   have placed them and denying it.

– Disconnecting and hiding telephones.

PHYSICAL ABUSE

– Hitting, slapping.

– Pulling hair and other body parts.

– Using a weapon or threatening to use one.

– Throwing objects toward or at me.

– Locking me out of the house.

– Choking, biting, kicking me.

– Refusing to help me when I am injured, sick, or
   pregnant.

– Depriving me of sleep.

– Turning out lights and leaving objects about so that I
   will be injured.

– Turning off the heat in the winter.

- Slamming doors and making other loud noises in the middle of a working night.
- Turning up the radio or television volume.

SEXUAL ABUSE

- Unwanted grabbing, rubbing, and pinching my body parts.
- Forced sex of any kind.
- Showing sexual interest in other women in public or private.
- Boasting about sexual affairs with other women.
- Withholding sex in an effort to punish me.
- Demanding sex when I am sick or after fighting with me.
- Making demeaning remarks about my body parts.
- Calling me derogatory sexual names like whore, bitch, or slut.
- Accusing my female friends of being lesbians with whom I'm having sex.
- Ignoring my refusal to have sex.
- Refusing intimacy.
- Demanding sex after staying out all night.
- Minimizing my feelings about sex.
- Criticizing my sexual performance and comparing it with other women.

Symptoms of Abuse in Children

Unexplained behavioral changes in a child signal that something is wrong, especially when the changes are abrupt. It is difficult for her to talk about sexual abuse because she is afraid and confused. Question a child's abrupt, unusual behavior changes. Ask:

- Has something happened to you that you are afraid to tell?
- Has someone touched or rubbed private parts of your body and told you not to tell?
- Who was it?
- Has anyone threatened to hurt or kill family members?
- What did they say?
- Have you ever awakened and found someone in bed with you who was not supposed to be there?
- Who was it?
- What did he or she say?
- What did he or she do?

On investigating illicit sexual activity experienced by a young child, direct questions will not always reveal the abuse immediately because the violator may be well known to her. Questions that probe indirectly are less threatening and can be followed later with more direct ones.

For more information, ask the child to draw a picture of

what happened to her. Remember that the story is more important than the quality of the drawing. Ask her to talk about the picture:

- Who is in it?

- What is happening?

- How is she feeling about the event?

- Who is not in the picture?

- Where are they?

- Where is help?

Women abused as children frequently complain that no one ever questioned them. Their sexual abuse left lasting negative impressions on them both as children and survivors.

Affirmations

During the course of therapy, books by women with similar life stories, poetry, and scriptural passages provided frames of reference for reflection, direction, and healing. They countered feelings of isolation, soothed, encouraged, and affirmed self-worth. The women also embraced ten principles that affirmed their ability to change.

1. I was born with authority.
2. I am never powerless because I can choose.

3. There are always options. I can identify and weigh them.

4. I choose best when I am clear about my options.

5. Freedom is my ability to choose how I will function in the world.

6. When another person chooses for me, I surrender my power to that person. When I choose, I reclaim my power.

7. I will take care of myself physically, mentally, and spiritually. One and a half won't do.

8. I can act on my decisions.

9. Small steps are manageable. Complete one small step before moving to another.

10. Success builds on itself and produces the results I choose.

Self-discovery with support stimulated the women to appreciate their qualities and feel better. Clarity about the issues helped them to identify alternatives and improve their judgments. However, wiser choices increased their confidence. They reclaimed their power and used it to take care of themselves without feeling guilty.

Planned attention to physical, mental, and spiritual development restored their balance and enabled them to manage stress. As the women realized their ability to create the results they wanted in their lives, they became stronger and motivated to move powerfully into the future.

The spiritual self-dimension emerged as the least developed and utilized. As with the physical and mental, when this dimension is underdeveloped or ignored, imbalance and inability to activate the full measure of our power result. Psalms and Proverbs proved to be good beginnings for stimulating thoughts about the women's existence and power.

Scripture helped to create new definitions. One passage offered meaningful direction. "Give, and it shall be given unto you; good measure, pressed down, and shaken together, and running over, shall men give into your bosom. For with the same measure that ye mete withal it shall be measured to you again." (Luke 6:38, KJV)

Giving and receiving are reciprocal processes that operate in our lives—in love, work, time, talent, money, and every other area. Our responses may be generous or stingy, depending on how much of ourselves we are willing to invest, but we get what we give. The principle is important because it helps to generate abundance in both our lives and those of others in our community.

Regular worship at church, prayer, Bible study, and meditation helped me to develop spiritually. I received guidelines, consolation, truth, and wisdom. Integrating one activity into my life before adding another allowed me to experience success. Success strengthened my faith and inspired me to give generously.

We are never confined to poverty in any area of our lives unless we internalize deprivation as a sole option. We adopt a poverty mentality when we perceive everything as a potential struggle and believe there is never enough of anything. By holding on so tightly to physical, emotional, and spiritual resources, it is no wonder that we receive even less in return.

Scripture confirms that we have these resources for a reason. While some may have more than others, our responsibility is to identify, appreciate, and use them. Misuse or neglect will decrease them and cause scarcity. Wise usage will increase our resources and create abundance. In all instances, we have choices.

As each of us understands that the package we came in is no mistake, our self-esteem will continue to grow. The capacity to choose is one of our most important human assets. Although disappointment and problems are a part of life, we can use our ability to choose to improve our circumstances and quality of life. We choose best when we are clear about the issues we face. This clarity helps us to name and examine the options that are always available. It is up to us to select the ones that are best for us. Always remember that choice is power because it allows us to create the results we want in our lives.

Therapists and Where to Find Them

About Psychotherapists (Therapists)

In most states, people may call themselves *therapists* without training, so the word does not give a thorough description of their
professional field or credentials. *Psychotherapists* are required to be
licensed and a member of a legitimate mental health profession.
Psychiatrists, clinical psychologists, social workers, nurse specialists, and pastoral and professional counselors are types of psychotherapists. Generally, the differences among them are in their
education and training programs.

Psychiatrists are physicians and therapists who can prescribe
medications. They have completed a three-year residency and additional supervised clinical training and experience in the diagnosis and treatment of mental, emotional, and behavioral disorders.

With some exceptions, physicians with additional training in psychoanalysis are known as psychoanalysts (also called analysts). All are required to be licensed in the state where they practice.

Clinical psychologists have earned doctoral degrees and supervised clinical training and experience in the diagnosis, treatment, and prevention of emotional and behavioral problems and mental disorders. Psychologists also administer and interpret psychological tests. They must have at least one year of postgraduate supervision—more in some states—and pass a licensing examination.

Clinical social workers have master's or doctoral degrees in social work and are required to complete two years of supervised social work practice in the diagnosis and treatment of psychosocial problems. Social work practice includes either casework, group work, or community organization services. Social workers extend treatment procedures to the home and community and must pass an examination to be licensed.

Clinical nurse specialists have master's or doctoral degrees in psychiatric mental health nursing. Two years of clinical experience in a specialty area under the supervision of a clinical nurse specialist are required. They must pass an examination in their specialty area to become certified.

Counselors have master's or doctoral degrees and supervised clinical experience in specialty areas. They are required to be licensed in many but not all states. *Marriage* and *family counselors* have training in marriage and family therapy and supervised clinical practice. Certified *pastoral counselors* have theology degrees, graduate study in the pastoral or a related field, and supervised clinical experience.

Where to Find Psychotherapists

You can find a psychotherapist (therapist) in several ways. Family physicians, pastors, and local and national mental health organizations are good referral sources for information. Friends and word-of-mouth recommendations are usually excellent sources. Good reputations follow good therapists. You can write or call for information from national organizations or consult your local telephone directory for local chapters.

AMERICAN ASSOCIATION OF PASTORAL COUNSELORS

9504A Lee Highway
Fairfax, Virginia 22031-2303
Phone: (703) 385-6967
Fax: (703) 352-7725
www.aapc.org

AMERICAN ASSOCIATION FOR MARRIAGE AND FAMILY THERAPY

1133 15th Street, NW, Suite 300
Washington, D.C. 20005-2710
Phone: (202) 452-0109
Fax: (202) 223-2329
www.aamft.org

AMERICAN COUNSELING ASSOCIATION

5999 Stevenson Avenue
Alexandria, VA 22304

Phone: (703) 823-9800

Fax: (703) 823-0252

www.counseling.org

AMERICAN GROUP PSYCHOTHERAPY ASSOCIATION

25 East 21st Street, 6th Floor

New York, NY 10010

Phone: (212) 477-2677 or (877) 668-2472

www.agpa.org

AMERICAN PSYCHIATRIC ASSOCIATION

1400 K Street, NW

Washington, DC 20005

Phone: (888) 357-7924

www.psych.org

AMERICAN PSYCHIATRIC NURSES ASSOCIATION

Colonial Place Three

2107 Wilson Boulevard, Suite 300-A

Arlington, VA 22201

Phone: (703) 243-2443

Fax (703) 243-3390

www.apna.org

AMERICAN PSYCHOLOGICAL ASSOCIATION

750 1st Street, NE

Washington, DC 20002-4242

Phone: (202) 336-5500 or (800) 374-2721

www.apa.org

ASSOCIATION OF BLACK PSYCHOLOGISTS

P.O. Box 55999

Washington, D.C. 20040-5999

Phone: (202) 722-0808

www.apsi.org

BLACK PSYCHIATRISTS OF AMERICA

P.O. Box 370659

Decatur, GA 30037

DEPRESSION AND RELATED AFFECTIVE DISORDERS ASSOCIATION

Meyer 3-181

600 North Wolfe Street

Baltimore, MD 21287-7381

Phone: (202) 955-5800 or (410) 955-4647

www.med.jhu.edu

NATIONAL ASSOCIATION OF BLACK SOCIAL WORKERS

www.nabsw.org

NATIONAL ASSOCIATION OF SOCIAL WORKERS

750 1st Street, NE, Suite 700

Washington, D.C. 20002-4241

Phone: (202) 408-8600 or (800) 638-8799

www.socialworkers.org

RAINN: RAPE, ABUSE, & INCEST NATIONAL NETWORK

635-B Pennsylvania Avenue, SE

Washington, D.C. 20003

Phone: (800) 656-HOPE, ext. 1

Fax: (202) 544-3556

rainnmail@aol.com

Bibliography

American Psychiatric Association. *Diagnostic and Statistical Manual of Mental Disorders* (4th Edition). Washington, D.C.: American Psychiatric Association, 1994.

Angelou, Maya. *And Still I Rise.* New York: Random House, Inc., 1978.

Angelou, Maya. *I Know Why the Caged Bird Sings.* New York: Random House, Inc., 1970.

Ball, Edward. *Slaves in the Family.* New York: Farrar, Straus and Giroux, 1998.

Bass, Ellen, and Laura Davis. *The Courage to Heal: A Guide for Women Survivors of Child Sexual Abuse.* New York: HarperCollins Publishers, 1988.

Beattie, Melody. *Codependent No More.* New York: Hazelden, 1987.

Cone, James H. *A Black Theology of Liberation.* Philadelphia and New York: J. B. Lippincott Company, 1970.

Davis, Angela. *Women, Race & Class.* New York: Vintage Books, 1988.

Dunbar, Paul Laurence. "We Wear the Mask." In Jay Martin and Gossie Hudson, eds. *The Paul Laurence Dunbar Reader.* New York: Dodd, Mead & Company, 1975.

Franklin, John Hope, and Alfred A. Moss Jr. *From Slavery to Freedom: A History of Negro Americans.* New York: Knopf, 1988.

Giddings, Paula. *When and Where I Enter.* New York: William Morrow and Company, 1984.

Green, Beverly. "African American Women." In Lillian Coman-Diaz and

Beverly Green, eds. *Women of Color: Integrating Ethnic and Gender Identities in Psychotherapy.* Boston, Massachusetts: Guilford Publications, Inc., 1994.

Grier, William H., and Price M. Cobb. *Black Rage.* New York: Basic Books, 1987.

Gutman, Herbert G. *The Black Family in Slavery and Freedom, 1750–1925.* New York: Pantheon Books, 1976.

Hine, Darlene Clark, and Kathleen Thompson. *A Shining Thread of Hope: A History of Black Women in America.* New York: Broadway Books, 1998.

Hooks, Bell. "Sexism and the Black Female Slave Experience and Continued Devaluation of Black Womanhood." In *Ain't I a Woman: Black Women and Feminism.* Boston, Massachusetts: South End Press, 1981.

Hurston, Zora Neale. *I Love Myself When I Am Laughing . . . And Then Again When I Am Looking Mean and Impressive.* Edited by Alice Walker. New York: The Feminist Press, 1979.

Johnson, Spencer, M.D. *Who Moved My Cheese?* New York: G. P. Putnam's Sons, Penguin Putnam, Inc., 1998.

McKinnon, Jesse. *The Black Population: 2000.* Census 2000 Brief. Current Population Reports, Series P20-530. Washington, D.C.: U.S. Government Printing Office, August 2001. Retrieved February 4, 2002, from the U.S. Census Bureau Web site: http://www.census.gov/prod/2001pubs/c2kbr01-5.pdf.

The Original African American Heritage Study Bible, King James Version. Nashville, Tennessee: The James C. Winston Publishing Company, 1993.

Rennison, Callie M. Intimate Partner Violence and Age of Victim, 1993–99, Special Report. Washington, D.C.: U.S. Department of Justice, Office of Justice Programs, Bureau of Justice Statistics, 2001. Retrieved February 4, 2002, from the Department of Justice Web site: http://www.ojp.usdoj.gov/bjs/pub/pdf/ipva99.pdf.

Stringer, Nelson H., M.D. *Uterine Fibroids: What Every Woman Needs to Know.* Glenview, Illinois: Physicians & Scientists Publishing Company, 1996.

Target Market News. The Buying Power of Black America (Annual Report, sixth ed.). Chicago: Target Market News, 1999.

U.S. Census Bureau. The Black Population in the United States (March 2001).

Current Population Survey (CPS) Reports: List of Tables (PPL–142). Table 7, Educational Attainment of the Population 25 Years and Over by Sex and Race and Hispanic Origin: March 2000, Female. Retrieved February 5, 2002, from the U.S. Census Bureau Web site: http://www.census.gov/population/socdemo/race/black/ppl–142/tab07.txt.

U.S. Census Bureau. The Black Population in the United States (March 2001). Current Population Survey (CPS) Reports: List of Tables (PPL–142). Table 11, Major Occupation Group of the Employed Civilian Population 16 Years and Over by Sex and Race and Hispanic Origin: March 2000, Female 2/. Retrieved February 4, 2002, from the U.S. Census Bureau Web site: http://www.census.gov/population/socdemo/race/black/ppl–142/tab11.txt.

U.S. Census Bureau. The Black Population in the United States (March 2001). Current Population Survey (CPS) Reports: List of Tables (PPL–142). Table 16, Poverty Status of the Population in 1999 by Age, Sex, and Race and Hispanic Origin, March 2000, Female 2/. Retrieved February 4, 2002, from the U.S. Census Bureau Web site: http://www.census.gov/population/socdemo/race/black/ppl–142/tab16.txt.

Villarosa, Linda, ed. *Body & Soul: The Black Women's Guide to Physical Health and Emotional Well-Being.* New York: HarperPerennial, 1994.

Walker, Lenore. *The Battered Woman.* New York: Springer, 1979.

White, Evelyn C. *Chain Chain Change: For Black Women Dealing with Physical and Emotional Abuse.* Seattle: Seal Press, 1985.

Wilson, Harriet E. *Our Nig; or, Sketches from the Life of a Free Black.* New York: Random House, Inc., 1983.

Wyatt, Gail E. *Stolen Women: Reclaiming Our Sexuality, Taking Back Our Lives.* New York: John Wiley & Sons, Inc., 1997.

Young, Andrea. *Life Lessons My Mother Taught Me.* New York: Tarcher/Putman, a member of Penguin Putnam, Inc., 2000.

About the Author

D. KIM SINGLETON, ED.D., IS A LICENSED CLINICAL PSY-
chologist, trainer, and motivational speaker. She maintains a large
private practice where she focuses on mood and anxiety disorders and Black women's issues. The recipient of a doctorate from
George Washington University, Dr. Singleton has made more than
eight hundred public appearances as a seminar leader, trainer, and
speaker. Dr. Singleton is the mother of a daughter and two sons.
She and her husband live in Maryland.